Rare Iron:

Two Undefeated Teams, Two Heisman Finalist~

and A Legacy in th

Jamie Jeffreys

Table of Contents

Copyright

ISBN: 9798823798990

Cover art designed and created by Graham Barley

Dedication

To the Men of the 1971 Alabama Crimson Tide football team, those that wore the uniform, those that guided their season, those that kept them healthy, recover from the rigors of playing major college football, progressing towards their academic goals, or centered and balanced mentally, spiritually, or emotionally. I have been graced with the opportunity to peak behind the curtain and have come to possess a deep and profound respect and admiration for not only what they did and endured, but the bond that unites them to this day, and the manner in which they use the lessons of that time to maintain their close fellowship, but to positively affect that world around them. They are a special and unique group, and I hope this book helps others appreciate how much they set the standard that carries Crimson Tide football even through today. I salute you all, and you have my respect and admiration.

Prelude

On November 27, 1971, two undefeated and untied college football teams thundered onto the artificial turf of Birmingham's Legion Field. There, within the confines of the "Old Gray Lady" on Fairmont Avenue, they would play for an undefeated season, a Southeastern Conference championship, a chance to contend for a mythical national championship in their upcoming bowl game, and possibly, the control of not only their shared state but Southern football in general.

Alabama had been the standard in the 1960s, but as the previous decade drew to a close, the mighty Tide had faltered to 6-5 and 6-5-1 seasons, which had not only affected recruiting and public perception, but had also created a growing chorus of whispers that maybe Coach Paul Bryant had reached his peak and was beginning the descent from the greatness that was the fate of almost every coach. Three championships in the sixties were remarkable, and there was certainly a valid argument for not only a fourth in 1966 but a completed run of three in a row. The string of All-Americans and household names like Stabler, Namath, and Jordan was second to none.

However, the very nature of college football leads to a "what have you done for me lately" mentality, and the trend seemed decidedly downward for Alabama by the time the Tide trudged off the Astrodome field after a feckless 24-24 tie with Oklahoma at the end of the 1970 season.

Auburn, on the other hand, had struggled for much of the previous decade, with a couple of bright-spot seasons like 1963 sprinkled in. That all began to change with the arrival of the dynamic duo of quarterback Pat Sullivan and receiver Terry Beasley on the Plains. Auburn, and coach Ralph Jordan, surrounded the pair with some other gifted offensive skill players, a rugged offensive line, and an opportunistic and big-play defense and the Tigers began to show their stripes. An 8-3 season in 1969, followed by a 9-2 record in 1970 seemed to herald a new promise of Auburn prominence, and with the supposed decline of their Crimson rivals, the time seemed ripe for the Tigers to grasp the seat at the head of the table.

Jordan was always one for innovation and trying something new, and with Sullivan, Beasley, and the chronically underappreciated Dick Schmalz, whose toughness and physicality made a perfect complement for the more mercurial and technical Beasley, he had the building blocks of something special. Along with running backs Terry Henley,

7

Harry Unger, and Tommy Lowry, the Auburn offense became a, for the time, high-wire, big-play, high risk-high reward unit that piled up big numbers often and sometimes came apart like a poorly maintained machine. But, Sullivan was tough, smart, and gritty, and would compete up to the final gun every Saturday, and the effect of his personality, charisma, and derring-do gave promise for attracting more talented and gifted players down the road and making a serious and plausible run at the top of the SEC, and maybe the nation.

While the Tigers seemed set on a style and a concept, Alabama was undergoing a seismic change in terms of offense. After two seasons of watching Scott Hunter shatter passing records at the Capstone, and Johnny Musso shine running and catching the ball out of the backfield while the record hovered just above .500, Bryant had had enough. Though Hunter absorbed much of the blame from fans and pundits, he played at a high level and under considerable pressure as the once stingy Alabama defense showed more cracks than the Jonestown dam. His successes were memorable, none more so than a 33-32 vanquishing of Southern legend Archie Manning and his Ole Miss Rebels in 1969 when both passers lit up the sky like the Battle of Britain. Musso was magnificent, there was talent at running back and some exceptional young offensive linemen, and there was potential on the defensive side of the ball, but the pro-style balanced attack was not working.

So, in the summer of 1971, after some soul-searching and secretive discussions with his coaching cronies, Bryant made the fateful and risky decision to chuck the offense that had rung up numbers but not wins and to switch to the wishbone. Spring training had shown that the best leader at quarterback was Terry Davis, a smaller, quicker athlete with a competitive nature, an elusive style, and an average arm. The wishbone put a premium on smarts, discipline, consistency, and leadership, along with toughness both physical and mental, and Davis had all of those in abundance.

Additionally, the wishbone allowed the Tide to maximize their depth at running back and in the offensive line, regain the ability to control the ball and the clock in critical times of the game, and gave Bryant and his staff the means to play to their strengths, especially in terms of field position and game control. It additionally gave him time to make the subtle changes on defense and to address the depth issues, because the offense kept the ball for long stretches, limiting the number of snaps the defense had to play.

So, on that partly cloudy day in the "Football Capital of the South", the white-clad Crimson Tide faced off against the boys-in-blue Tigers with state, conference, and regional supremacy on the line, with the legacy of a legendary coach at stake, and with a multitude of personal and program storylines in play. Alabama entered the game as the third-ranked team in the nation, Auburn checked in at number five, and with bowl games already locked in against Nebraska in Miami and Oklahoma in New Orleans respectively, they both had legitimate national championship aspirations. As of 2020, the two teams have met some eighty-five times, but in 1971, for the only time so far, they were both undefeated, untied, and, like Frost, standing at a dividing place in their respective paths as programs. Who would use the momentum of that day as a springboard to greater things? It is unlikely that anyone there, whether participant or observer, understood just how impactful that game would turn out to be, but even that day, there was a special feel in the air. There are many unusual occurrences and strange happenings in this historic and highly contested series, but in that magical season, the rarest of all games occurred, and with it, two teams, two coaches, and two programs took the first steps down separate and significant pathways. In 1971, on the artificial surface of Legion Field, it was not just a football game, not even just another Iron Bowl, but something rarer, something more special and lasting. It was Rare Iron.

Two Stars in an Alabama Sky

So many storylines. Let's start with the battle between two high school legends, two schoolboys whose exploits at Banks High School and John Carrol Catholic School thrilled their fans and neighbors, inspired the attention of football followers outside of their native Birmingham, and attracted the best sales pitches of college coaches throughout the South. Johnny Musso of the Banks Jets, a slashing powerful running back with a good burst of speed and uncanny balance, and Pat Sullivan of the John Carrol Catholic Cavaliers with his exceptional athleticism, lightning arm, and talent for improvisation and saving the day, were the crown jewels of the 1967 recruiting classes in the state of Alabama, and the fondest dream of every college coach in the region was to land them both. A backfield of Sullivan and Musso looked like a surefire winner and maybe a championship contender, and the inability to land at least one of them would be a serious blow to either of the primary state schools.

Musso's time at Banks High School not only made him a legend in Alabama High School Football but helped form the player and the man he would display during his four years at the Capstone. In an <u>Alabama Newscenter</u> interview done by

Wayne Hester published on May 12, 2017, Musso would recall the impact his time as a Jet would have on him.

"Oh, my goodness," Musso said of his time at Banks, "four great years. What really stands out is when Coach White came over to the freshman field late in the season and started coaching me. I only weighed 125 pounds, but after lifting weights and training I made the varsity as a sophomore. With players like Billy Strickland, Johnny Johnston, and Sam Chambliss, we won the state championship."

It wasn't only his time on the playing fields that helped to mold him. There were plenty of influences, from a variety of sources, that prompted him to become a success both on the field and off. From the same interview;

"He recalled his math teacher, Rosemary Buettner, a mentor who 'saw stuff in me that I didn't see, and I wanted to live up to her expectations.'

Musso even remembered Birmingham News sportswriters from back in the day, calling the names of Alf Van Hoose, Jimmy Bryan, and Clyde Bolton.

When asked about the second effort he displayed as a running back, Musso said it came from his mother, Josie. 'She had a hard life,' he said, 'She was tough. Putting forth your best effort was just expected.'"

Sullivan's high school days also contain the seeds of the premiere player and successful coach he would become. In an interview with al.com's Gary Eastwick, published on October 7th of 2016, and updated May 18, 2019, on the occasion of the dedication of the playing field at John Carrol in his honor, Sullivan recalled those days.

"Sullivan was a three-sport star at John Carroll before embarking on a college career at Auburn, highlighted by the 1971 Heisman Trophy Award. While football may have been his best sport, it was far from his only sport. 'Some of my fondest memories were playing other sports,' he said.

Sullivan recalled his freshman, sophomore, and junior years at John Carroll; on most days, he did not leave the campus until the evening. He'd spend the afternoons playing in a game, or practicing. 'As soon as football (season) was over, I'd go straight into basketball. As soon as basketball was over, I'd go to spring training (football). As soon as that was over, I'd go to baseball. And as soon as baseball was over, school was over with."

But, it wasn't just the coaching staff at John Carroll that helped to shape the future Heisman winner and the man who would impact so many lives as a coach himself. From the same interview, Sullivan discussed his family.

"I was very fortunate with my parents. My mother, she worked just to take her whole paycheck to put us through a Catholic (school) education. And my dad was a service man for the gas company; worked all the time.

We were a close family. I think the thing that we all learned was how to work hard. We learned what was important. Our faith was important to our family."

Eventually, Musso would choose to go to Tuscaloosa and Sullivan would opt for Auburn, but their careers would be, at some level, forever linked. Both established backroom legends during Freshman games since they weren't allowed to play varsity games in their first seasons under the rules of the day, and both had highlights and acclaim as sophomores and juniors, but always Sullivan, by virtue of being a quarterback, by his more naturally charismatic public persona, and by the result of the perception of a surging Tiger program borne out by the seventeen wins, seemed to be a step above, a more polished and promising player, and the recipient of more national acclaim.

In fact, Sullivan had become, to Alabama fans in fancy if not in fact to Bryant and his staff, the personal and ever-present demon that haunted their football dreams. From leading a late and dramatic comeback in a JV game to superb individual performances in 1969's 49-26 drubbing followed by a gut-punch 33-28 comeback in 1970 after Hunter and the Tide had surged to an early 17-0 lead, he was the program's arch-nemesis. They simply couldn't stop him when he got on a roll, and Beasley seemed to be on the receiving end of many of his strikes, outmaneuvering the defensive backs or simply displaying a greater commitment to snatching the ball out of the air in a contested situation. Alabama's offense enjoyed significant success against the Plainsmen defense, but nothing and nobody could seemingly top the flamboyant Sullivan.

It was Musso, however, who was bestowed with the imaginative and memorable nickname. Known as the "Italian Stallion", he combined a slashing and physical running style with deceptively quick feet and incredible balance. He had a talent for avoiding contact at the last minute, spinning, using the "dead leg" technique, or subtly shifting his weight or footing to leave a diving defender clutching only air. During his entire career he displayed a knack for finding the end zone, leading the SEC in rushing touchdowns and points in 1971, while also leading the SEC in rushing yards in both 1970 and 1971, and yards from scrimmage in both years as well. For all of Hunter's pyrotechnics, Musso was the heart and soul of the offense, the most consistent weapon in the arsenal, and a fan favorite, as well as sharing a special bond with his gruff head coach. In my previous work, *Crimson Fraternity,* I shared a story about how his teammates chose to send him to see Bryant with a request to be allowed to wear their hair at a more fashionable and modern length. The team, or at least those who desired to follow the current trend, was not very optimistic about a positive response from the Coach, but they felt that at least the popular Musso would not be punished for asking.

As the 1971 season unfolded, it became apparent that however accomplished and acclaimed the two had been in the previous seasons, they were both determined to take things to an entirely new level for their senior seasons. Musso, as has been mentioned, would lead the SEC in rushing yards, rushing touchdowns yards from scrimmage, and points, and would be fourth in the conference in total touchdowns responsible for. When you review the articles of the day or watch some of the highlight packages of that season, you run across references to how the switch to the wishbone probably cost Musso carries and yards and hampered his production, but his rushing yards and yards from scrimmage decreased only slightly while rushing touchdowns and points increased significantly. Musso and his backfield mates LaBue, Bisceglia, Beck, and Jackson adapted to the new offense with gusto, not only running the ball with passion and success but blocking for each other unselfishly and sharing the load without few, if any, complaints. Winning outstripped statistics, and after two subpar seasons, it was ambrosia.

However, while the number of carries and overall touches were more dispersed and divided, Musso doubled the accumulated yards of any other back, and almost tripled the touchdown numbers. He did more with less, and when the need was greatest, the ball found its way to his arms as it always had. He rode the Tide's success and his readily apparent ability and production to a fourth-place finish in the Heisman race, and an All-American designation. Additionally, his selfless nature and willingness to block for the other backs, a trait that was widespread among the entire backfield and especially true of fellow starter Joe LaBue, made him even more popular with not only the coaching staff and his teammates, but the fan base as well. I, like many fans of the era, have an almost permanent mental highlight package featuring Musso fighting through arm tackles, tear-away jersey streaming away leaving opponents grasping red shreds, driving forward carrying multiple tacklers for that extra yardage, or diving the last few yards into paydirt.

A couple of quotes from a Pat Putnam article in the October 11, 1971 edition of *Sports Illustrated* entitled "Pride in the Red Jersey" give a real insight into how Coach Bryant viewed his star running back.

"Johnny can do everything. He's a great runner, blocker, and passer. If we let him, he'd be a great defensive back too. Last year (1970) he had to run his own interference and he still gained over 1,100 yards. The ideal situation would be Musso running with Musso up front blocking for him."

Later in the same article, which went to press after a convincing 48-23 victory over an Ole Miss team known for its offensive prowess in which Musso had helped steady the offense after an injury to Terry Davis pushed little-used Butch Hobson, better known for his subsequent baseball career, into the triggerman position, by rushing for 193 yards on 22 carries, Bryant offered what for him might have been the ultimate praise available to a runner.

"I don't know which I like best. Watching Musso run or watching him block. He simply wipes out people when he blocks."

Sadly, however, the narrative heading into the 1971 Iron Bowl game was not centered on Musso's heroics, his high Heisman finish, or the culmination of a celebrated career, but on the status of his toe. Musso had sustained an injury to his right big toe, what we would now define as a "turf toe injury" which is not only very painful but almost debilitating to a running back. Turf toe is a sprain of the ligaments around the big toe joint, usually caused by overuse in flexing the joint under the weight of the body. During the artificial turf era of football, it was more common, as the hard undersurface prevented the normal flexion of the foot during play, but even today, with the concurrent advances in sports medicine and its treatments and equipment, the injury can have a major effect on players, their seasons, and in some cases, careers. In the leadup to the game, Musso's condition was severe enough to warrant crutches for the past three weeks and there was a general consensus that his playing status was questionable at best.

Riding to the rescue of Alabama and their championship dreams was the unlikely duo of Jim Goostree and Sang Lyda. The Alabama head trainer and his assistant, who would become legends in their own rights, had watched the All-American halfback torture himself trying to get ready to play. The difficult task of watching him hobble through practice and treating his pain and discomfort afterward had exhausted their normal treatment protocols, and it was going to take something very special, and probably highly creative, to turn an effective "Stallion" loose on a vulnerable Tiger defense and to give the Tide their best chance of remaining undefeated and facing the powerful Cornhuskers for a potential National Championship.

Goosetree, after exploring several options, settled on treatment and an oversized shoe for the injured appendage modified to give the toe more room without allowing the foot to slide around. He addressed possible blister issues by cutting it down slightly and restitching the resulting hybrid and utilized trial-and-error experimentation with a combination of tongue depressors and a metal centerpiece taped together and inserted underneath the affected joint, which allowed Musso to run fairly normally without the injured toe being rolled into contact with the bottom of the shoe, which would have aggravated the injury.

When the proper combination was found, the halfback was able to take the field for this last battle against Sullivan and his Auburn teammates. While the device and the modified shoe allowed him to play, it was his own high tolerance for pain and his desire to "do his part" for his teammates and his school that drove Musso to not only take the field but to excel in this showdown game. He would rush the ball 33 times, many in the second half when the Tide needed to keep the ball and bleed the clock, gaining 167 yards, an astounding 5.1 yards a carry. If the injury had kept him from playing, Johnny Musso would have been an Alabama legend for all that he had done before, but this game, and his herculean effort, would ensure that his name would be a permanent part of Crimson Tide lore.

Sullivan, on the other hand, would be held in check. Bryant had hired secondary coach Bill "Brother" Oliver, a man who would feature in many big games both in this series, and in major victories for both schools over a distinguished career, as well as being a starter on the 1961 national championship squad, and his secondary, aided by an aggressive philosophy that continually got defenders into Sullivan's face and forced him away from his timing routes, finally held the prolific passer in check.

In the "Pride in the Red Jersey" article, Bryant noted Oliver's contribution in this manner.

"You can give a lot of credit for our secondary to Bill Oliver. He taught us some new techniques and gave our people more confidence."

While Sullivan, at roughly six feet tall, was not "short" by any measure, the Tide defense made his vision an issue in this game. The Auburn offense featured a mixture of timing routes and the ability of he and Beasley to visually cue each other and adjust to what they were seeing. The interior pressure prevented a lot of this, and Alabama's mixture of man-help and zone defenses took away some of Beasley's medium routes, where he was so effective in using his strength and body control to hold off individual defenders and not only make catches but gain valuable yards after the reception. While Sullivan, who was a three-sport athlete in high school good enough to garner college offers in all three, was a creative and effective scrambler, Alabama displayed defensive discipline and dominance at the line of scrimmage, which meant when Sullivan did pull the ball down to seek yards or passing lanes, the three starting linebackers, Rouzie, Strickland, and Surlas, was either available to track him down or were in his secondary passing lanes.

In holding Sullivan to around 50% as a passer, with no touchdowns and two interceptions, (the one Auburn touchdown would come on a halfback pass from Harry Unger to Beasley) and by shutting the Tiger running game down to a large degree, the Alabama defense muted the talented Auburn quarterback and his uncanny receiver and forced the Tigers to work hard for every yard gained. There is no disputing Sullivan's ability and his penchant for leadership and effort, but by controlling the clock with over forty minutes of possession and by establishing not only the tempo of the game, but its mode as well, Alabama put the game into the hands of its improved defense, the triple option magic of its gritty and talented quarterback, and the injured but proud star running back who gutted his way to a starring performance.

Ultimately, like most football games among teams with comparable talent bases, the contest was won and lost at the line of scrimmage, and it was there, on both sides of the battle, that Alabama was able to effectively dominate Auburn. The ability to control the game tempo and the clock for the wishbone, and the simple fact that the Tide defensive line was consistently winning their individual and group battles against the Tiger offensive line, allowed Alabama to play the game the way they wanted to, and to prevent Sullivan, Beasley and

24

the Auburn running backs who could not match Musso, Bisceglia and LaBue stat for stat, but were effective and versatile in their own rights, from establishing any sort of rhythm and consistency on offense. Sullivan had established a well-earned reputation for playing within the offense until the opportune or needful moment when he stepped outside of it and pulled a rabbit out of his white helmet, but, like any quarterback, no matter how talented and determined, when forced to do so play after play, mistakes and inaccuracies crept in.

The combination of scheme, coaching, and the continued rise of the wishbone effect left the Heisman Trophy winner confused, battered, and ultimately ineffective, and the day, wrapped in Crimson, would belong to the hobbled but gutty Musso in this, the last of their head-to-head meetings.

However, a standing memorial to both of these extraordinary players is that the mention of their names, or the invoking of the era, brings memories of their exploits and their character freshly to the minds of those who experienced southern football in the day, or those who study the past and appreciate greatness. The image of the two conversing after the game exhausted with their efforts and the long season, but both humble and truly appreciative of their gifts and the opportunities they had been given, is one of the lasting memories of my youngest day of fandom.

Terry Davis

"I would go to battle with that guy". In the football world, that phrase has a very specific meaning, and when applied to a quarterback, even more so. What it means in that context is that the individual in consideration has that special mix of leadership, charisma, and humanity that makes you identify with them, respect them, and feel vindicated in following them into a competitive situation with an expectation of success. After finishing my second interview with Mr. Davis, the first of which you can read in my previous book *Crimson Fraternity*, my wife approached me and asked me how it had gone. My response is quoted above, but I have heard the same phrase used about Terry by those who played with him or were associated with the team during his career. He was and is a Leader, and I can understand the effect he had in the huddle on those hot Alabama afternoons in the early 1970s.

In that earlier work, I gave each of the wishbone-era quarterbacks a nickname or moniker for their chapter, and for Terry Davis, it was quite easy. I referred to him as "The Engine" a concept that started with listening to John Forney talk about "little Terry Davis from Bogalusa, Louisiana" as the heartbeat of the Alabama wishbone offense. In those first few years, the offense was somewhat limited to a handful of running plays and even fewer passing plays, and it was often up to Davis to make the machine hum. The car doesn't run if the engine isn't performing at its peak, and Terry Davis did just that with regularity.

Growing up in Louisiana, not far from Baton Rouge, he was a Tiger fan, especially of LSU quarterback Nelson Stockley. He told me in our previous interview that he was not one who watched a lot of football on television, preferring to play, but he did make time to watch Stockley and the Tigers. Under the tutelage of his high school coach Tommy Leos, he was highly proficient in an offense built around his skills, with roll-outs and bootlegs, getting him on the edge of the defense with the option of running with his quickness and toughness or throwing with exceptional accuracy on the run to the open receivers. When we talked, I mentioned that, in watching the available video of his career at Alabama, I was struck by his accuracy in rolling to his left, and his compact and repeatable throwing motion. For most right-handed quarterbacks, it is a difficult thing to master, rolling left with speed and then throwing with accuracy, and usually requires the player to take an extra step and gather himself, as well as rotate his shoulders to get the ball into a throwing position. If you watch Davis at Alabama, he threw the ball from his shoulder with no wind-up and did not require the gather step, making the throw quicker and harder to defend. I asked him about this, and he remembered a drill Coach Leos had used in his high school day, in which the quarterbacks knelt on one knee, then picked the ball up, brought it to the shoulder, and delivered it quickly and efficiently. Like so many lessons he learned from Coach Leos, it was a lesson that stayed with him.

There were other hallmarks in his high school career that would establish a pattern for what was to come. One that he specifically mentioned, and a topic we will cover later in this chapter, was his knack for outplaying more heralded opposing quarterbacks. In a high school playoff game, Davis and his teammates faced off against future Arkansas and Buffalo Bills starter Joe Ferguson, and, in his own words, "I was pretty pleased with that result". Competitive to the max, Terry Davis would rise to the occasion time and time again in Tuscaloosa.

It wasn't easy. He arrived just as the Tide began to turn away from their I-formation, play-action past towards a more pro-style, wide-open passing attack that best-suited starter Scott Hunter. It produced records in passing and high point totals, but not as much success on the scoreboard, and heading into the spring of 1971, there were a handful of contenders, including future starter Gary Rutledge.

When I asked Terry about that period, and his frame of mind, he referenced a combination of experience and limited success in limited opportunities, as a belief in his ability. "I had a knack for moving the offense. I thought if the offense was the right one for me, I could be very successful, and that would make the team successful."

It wasn't just a personal feeling. He had enjoyed a few moments in the sun during his time as a backup, especially a performance against Florida in leading the team to a score, an event that led to one even more important in the long term. "I was in the TV room watching the 'Bear Bryant' show after the Florida game my sophomore year. After showing the touchdown drive that I had led, they came back to Coach Bryant, and he said, 'That's Terry Davis from Bugaloosa, you folk's keep an eye on him, he's a winner'". That appellation, as many have mentioned, was the highest form of praise from the legendary coach, and to hear it as a sophomore, one who was not yet a starter was a nugget of positivity that would buoy his spirits through some of the stormy times ahead.

Terry would admit to me that he knew about his advantages, but he still didn't yet have the confidence that he would become known for. The offense in the Spring was still primarily what the team had run under Hunter, and he knew it wasn't the best fit for his skills. What he couldn't know, as he worked through the summer painting goalposts and honing his conditioning and skills, was that a major change was on the horizon.

In spite of the consecutive six-win seasons, which led to discomfort and unhappiness for the players and coaches, and more overt emotions for the fanbase accustomed to success and championships, there was a strong base of talent. There were several excellent backs, led by the multi-talented Musso and the versatile and under-appreciated LaBue, some very special if still young offensive linemen like Hannah and Brown, and quality wideouts led by David Bailey. The defense had been far below the Alabama standard, but an infusion of younger players and a couple of key coaching additions that we will highlight later held promise if the offense could be productive and give them time to develop. What was needed was a way of re-asserting the game control and physicality on offense that Bryant preferred, and as they assembled for their first team meeting in the fall, the coach unveiled his plan.

It was the "sink-or-swim" meeting, and Davis was excited by the end. "It was both a shock and a relief. It suited our talent, the multiple talented running backs, and the ability at receiver. It would put me on the run, let me play on the edge of the defense, and make decisions. I had seen the wishbone, even though I didn't at that time know all the mechanics of playing quarterback in it, but it put the quarterback on the move and making decisions every play. I thought it would suit me. The first year was very basic, option, counter plays, and a couple of power plays. We worked against our defense, one of the toughest we faced, but we had success. By the time we went to Los Angeles, I felt confident about the offense and what I needed to do but was worried about beating those guys. They were good."

The USC game will most likely always live in Alabama football lore, but there were others in that '71 season that also stand out to Davis. He was quick to mention, as are many of his teammates, the Houston game, one that is often lost among the memories of that season for most fans. The Cougars, featuring three future NFL players in Robert

Newhouse, Riley Odoms, and Willie Roberts on offense, and highly respected coach Bill Yeoman calling the plays were explosive and the game was an offensive shootout with the Tide finally prevailing 34-20. Both defenses struggled with the other's option attack, and the game was entertaining to watch and tough to play.

As always, the Tennessee game that season was a measuring stick, especially for Terry and the offense as the Volunteers featured a rugged, physical defense led by an experienced linebacker corp. Even tougher for the quarterback, on a personal level, was the trip to Baton Rouge to face his childhood favorite LSU. "Growing up about 100 miles from Baton Rogue, that game was always going to be big for me, and that first year, I don't think I played very well. The stadium is very loud, the fans are always into the game, and I didn't execute that well. I let it get to me some, maybe trying too hard and being impatient, but the team picked me up and we got a big win."

Ole Miss, which was the game that generated the *Sports Illustrated* article that I have cited several times, saw Musso and LaBue have big games, and Davis played very well until suffering an injury that removed him from the game for a significant time. "Against Florida, I had bruised my shoulder.

I wasn't big enough to run over anybody, but I tried to bulldoze a defensive back and he knocked me out of bounds and I lost feeling in the shoulder for a while. I took therapy and it was getting some better, but I reinjured it against Ole Miss, and also got hit hard in the hip on an option play. I knew it hurt but didn't realize it was really injured until later. Coach Goostree wanted to shoot me up, and I fought him because I don't like shots. The hip wasn't a real problem, but the shoulder lingered the rest of the season."

It was in Birmingham, against the highly-rated Tigers and their Heisman Trophy winner Pat Sullivan, that Davis would once again show the ability to elevate his game, and in so doing elevate the team around him. In the next season, he would do the same to fellow Louisianian Bert Jones, whose Heisman hopes and his team's national title dreams both evaporated in the heat of Legion Field as Davis would pass and run and fake and pitch and lead his Crimson Tide to a convincing 35-21 win. It took a bit of asking, but he finally admitted that he did take some pleasure in those matchups and in performing well.

"Any competitor wants to play better against top competition. I wanted to show what I could do against them. If I had gone to LSU, then I would have been competing against Bert to be the starter, and the same if Pat had come to Alabama."

He added a little story that might help those who haven't had the pleasure of meeting him or talking to him to see how he viewed such competition. "I went out for the coin toss in '72 against Bert and LSU. After the toss, I turned back and shook his hand, and said 'Bert, have a good game'. He just looked confused, probably thought I was crazy, but I meant it. I wanted him to play his best, and then to play my best and be better for my team."

And it was the team that mattered most to Terry Davis. "It was an honor to play against Pat, and I always liked Bert Jones. For me, I just wanted to do my part. The team wins, anything else is just extra."

That cloudy day in Legion Field, it was about the team, but it was old number 10 that led the charge. When I asked about the game plan and if there were any special things that they had prepared for Auburn, he said the offense was still pretty basic, the key was to read the defense and execute. Under Coach Bryant and Coach Moore, it was about preparation. During the pre-game, the conversation among the coaches and quarterbacks was always the same. "Do you know what you are going to do if you get ahead, or if you get behind? Do you have a plan?"

There were two key things that really resonate if you watch the game. The first was a little planned wrinkle, "breaking" the wishbone and splitting LaBue out behind the wide receiver. The threat of Musso and the ability to still run option plays, as well as the attention drawn by Bailey running deep, left the halfback alone in the flats, and he was on the receiving end of three big completions, using his running skills to maximize the gains and keep the sticks moving. It was something new and used to great advantage.

The other thing I noticed was an adjustment early in the game to feature more counter option. There were two basic types of this play, in which the quarterback and sometimes one or more backs, start in one direction, then spin 180 degrees and run the play in the opposite. Auburn had decided to defend the triple option with their linebackers being the pitch read key and a player standing up was a more difficult read. Also, the Tiger defense was best when it was in pursuit, using its quickness as an asset, and the counter option turned this to an Alabama advantage, slowing down the pursuit and creating some indecision and lack of execution. Early in the game, Davis was the primary ball carrier, with the threat of

Musso drawing defenders into conflict, but later, after his two touchdowns and early success, Musso found himself with room to run on the play, as Alabama rode the play and others to a two-to-one time of possession advantage, a key component in keeping the explosive Sullivan-Beasley combo at bay.

The win, and the season as a whole, is in no way diminished by the outcome of the Orange Bowl. Davis said the only regret was that he felt Alabama didn't play its best game, didn't make the game a contest for sixty minutes, but the effects of that season still resonate for him personally, and maybe even more in terms of being a part of a team of guys who worked so hard, survived so much, and brought the Alabama program back to the standard that had been established in the 1960s.

"Certainly, that season was a catalyst to what came later. Two subpar seasons, subpar for what Alabama was used to, meant it was time to start on a new path. Coach Bryant was a winner, and he was going to make changes until he found ways for us to be winners. We had depth at running back and some really good linemen. I think he won something like 110 games in the wishbone era. If he had retired in 1970, he would have been known as a great coach, but to make changes, to find a way to play his kind of football, to win three more national championships just served to enhance his legacy.

There were about thirteen of us who finished out of that big class I came in with, and we played a part in bringing the Alabama program back again, back where it belonged. It was a great thrill and honor to play on those teams, with those coaches and those guys. We are still close. I have great friendships and memories. When we get together, those gatherings and the conversations we have are sweet."

I mentioned the term "standard". It comes up a lot around Alabama football, one of many commonalities between the Bryant years and the current run of success under Coach Nick Saban. But, it is also a term that gets used a lot when you talk to others about Terry Davis. Time and again, teammates and observers from the day refer to his setting the standard for what a wishbone quarterback was and how he should play. When I asked about this, I knew he would be reluctant to answer, because he truly does not like to talk much about himself apart from his team. But, he did give me this answer.

"I appreciate you saying that, and those others who felt that way. If I did that, it was because as a team we were good. I had to play at a high standard because I was surrounded by great players. They were really good, and I owed it to them to play good. Look at the guys I played with. So many of them set the standard for how to play their position, for how to do it the Alabama way."

Two Men with the Vision

For Alabama Crimson Tide fans who became aware of the program anywhere from the mid-1970s through today, the notion that there was ever a period in which there was a growing consensus that the game had probably passed by Paul "Bear" Bryant, and that his Alabama program was headed towards the mediocre region of SEC football, and possibly lower in terms of regional and national perception, probably seems ludicrous and fanciful. However, as the 1971 season began its approach during the summer months preparatory to the beginning of fall camp, that was the perception that was gaining some momentum among not only rival fan bases and sports editors, but Alabama fans as well. As Bryant approached his 60s, many thought his best days were behind him, and the glories of the 1960s were the high-water mark for his tenure at the Capstone.

There was some evidence that such believers could point to. From 1961-1966, Alabama had accumulated three national championships of recognizable merit (in that day of championships voted on by various groups and organizations, there were several such championships awarded in any season, but there were three or maybe four that were considered widely accepted and recognized) and, infamously, had been denied such recognition with what might have been his most complete and dominate team in 1966 when an undefeated and untied Alabama squad that surrendered only 4.0 points per game and dominated some quality football teams, was only deemed to be the third-best team behind a once-tied and bowl absent Notre Dame squad who had tactically agreed to a 10-10 tie with Michigan State in terrible weather and field conditions so that neither would suffer a mistake-driven loss. That topic has been fully and professionally covered in other works, but the argument for that team, and the 1962 squad led by future NFL Hall-of-Famer Lee Roy Jordan and sophomore sensation and future Hall-of-Famer Joe Namath which suffered a tough and somewhat controversial 7-6 loss to Georgia Tech early in the season and finished with a 17-0 victory over a highly regarded Oklahoma squad and its legendary coach Bud Wilkinson, in a game that saw Jordan record an astonishing 31 tackles and Namath surgically dissect a proud Sooner defense, all of this in Miami under the gaze of President John Kennedy, could and certainly have been made for such consideration. Even the two-loss team of 1963, by a combined six points, was a legitimate high-quality team.

However, starting in 1968, the run began to lose steam. The season itself was a "close call", two losses to Ole Miss 8-10, and Tennessee 9-10 which were not danger signs in themselves, but the fact that Ole Miss, not known as a physically dominant team, was able to match Alabama blow for blow was. Then came the almost complete domination of the Tide in a 35-10 Gator Bowl loss that wasn't as close as the score. The next season did not see a return to the Bama standard of the decade, a 6-5 record made worse by a 2-4 slate in conference. A loss to Vandy, another loss, this one a thumping, by Tennessee, and a blowout defeat to Auburn 49-26 led to an embarrassing 47-33 loss to Colorado in the Liberty Bowl. Even Scott Hunter's aerial wizardry and the emergence of Musso could not salvage what seemed a lost season to many observers and fans, and the past two season's gradual increase in opponent scoring average suddenly ballooned at a double rate to 24.4 points a game, almost unfathomable for a Bryant coached team. In an attempt to adapt to the changing nature of the game and the growth of the passing game, Alabama had adopted a more open, pro-style attack with a lot of medium depth routes and more deliberate deep shots, which resulted in significant growth in passing yards and explosive plays, but also in a loss of game control and field position dominance, hallmarks of the Bryant style.

Things only got worse in 1970. Turnovers grew alarmingly, the defensive woes remained, and inconsistency and uncertainty in the offensive line led to a "feast or famine" offense that spluttered too often when it was needed. The only bright spot was Musso, who exhibited his All-American credentials. The season included a crushing 42-21 loss to USC in Birmingham that was more dominating than the final score, as Sam "Bam" Cunningham ran roughshod, and embarrassing losses to Tennessee and Ole Miss. The final indignity was a 33-28 loss to Auburn, in which the Tide had an early 17-0 lead and watched it evaporate in the brilliance of Sullivan and Beasley. A Bluebonnet Bowl tie with Oklahoma left the Crimsons battered, bruised, and bewildered, and a lot of outsiders convinced that the storied run was over and that maybe it was time for Bryant to consider the NFL or maybe even retirement to the Athletic Director's job.

On the opposite side of the state, Ralph "Shug" Jordan was enjoying a bit of a renaissance on the Plains. Shug was a decorated athlete at Auburn, graduating in 1932 as the Porter Cup winner at Auburn, recognized as the best All-Around athlete on the campus.

Jordan would be named the head basketball coach at Auburn, a position he would hold from 1933-1942, and then from 1945-1946, bookending his service in World War II in the US Army, seeing action in North Africa, earning a Purple Heart and a Bronze Star at Normandy, and later serving at Okinawa.

In 1946, Jordan would serve one season as an assistant for the Miami Seahawks of the All-American Football Conference, then four years as an assistant at the University of Georgia, where he also coached basketball. Finally, in 1951, he would return to his alma mater, becoming head football coach at Auburn, and would remain there until his retirement after the 1975 season. He remains the winningest coach at the school, and was a 1982 inductee into the College Football Hall of Fame.

During his long tenure at Auburn, he would experience several successful runs, including a National Championship in 1957 that was slightly tarnished by a probation caused by payments to two high school players. The 1958 team followed up that undefeated season with a 9-0-1 slate and an eight-win season in 1960 and a nine-win slate in 1963 thrilled win-hungry fans of the Tigers, and there were only a handful of poor seasons after his first two.

But, for all his relative success, he was relegated to second fiddle once the dominance of Bryant began to exert itself around 1960. Auburn was competitive in the SEC, qualified for a couple of bowl games, and certainly won some thrilling victories, but, as we have pointed out, Alabama was almost continually in the running for national consideration, and enjoyed a run of superior athletes, especially at quarterback with Trammell, Namath, Stabler, and Sloan. Alabama won the majority of recruiting battles in the state and the region, and the Tigers were in the position of looking up at their hated rivals.

1968 would be the key year for Auburn as well. The arrival of Pat Sullivan and Terry Beasley, and the decision to build an offense around them and their special connection and talents, produced a late-career renaissance for Jordan that gave him a final chance to change the narrative and get the last word on Bryant. Jordan, though a solid and fundamental coach, had a fondness for the flair and excitement of the trick play, the surprise package, and the explosive and unforeseen special teams gamble, and his coaching style was less authoritarian than the gruff and intimidating Tide headman. If Bryant on the field most resembled a John Wayne character, then Jordan was much more like Andy Griffith's Andy

45

Taylor. A strong and committed core encased in a folksy, cooperative exterior.

Now, with the blossoming talents of Sullivan and Beasley, he was ready to put the ball in their hands and take some chances. Even as freshmen, unable to play in varsity games by the rules of the day, they and their classmates were being groomed, and the offense was undergoing a transformation to take advantage of Sullivan's athleticism, tenacity, mid-level accuracy, and quick release, along with Beasley's route running and strength. There was, as usual, some talent on the Plains, and the excitement of nabbing Sullivan and his almost mythic status during his Freshman year started a resurgence that was timed beautifully with the decline in Tuscaloosa. 1968 brought about a 7-4 record capped with a Sun Bowl victory, and with Sullivan in the saddle, the Tigers surged to an 8-3 1969, complete with the throttling of Alabama that was not tarnished with a competitive Bluebonnet Bowl loss.

1970 brought about a high-flying and thrilling 9-2 result capped by the comeback against the Tide and a Gator Bowl victory. As the Tigers, and Jordan, looked ahead to 1971, there was a valid reason to believe that they were on the come and that the momentum and excitement of their success and their style of play, which was reaping rewards on the recruiting trail already, would help set the stage for a continuation of such even after Sullivan and Beasley took their talents on to the NFL.

For Bryant, this was the crux of the matter. It was not so much the personal challenge of Jordan and the Tiger's resurgent program, but the perception that they were just one of the regional, not to mention national, teams poised to not only pass Alabama but possibly bury them in the collective dust. College football played at the highest level, and for the ultimate prize, has much of the nature of a collection of prime predators. Weakness and vulnerability were rewarded with swarming ferocity and rabid destruction. Alabama, heading into the 1971 season looked vulnerable, and its storied coach could hear the wolves circling.

Again, quoting from the Putnam article "Pride in the Red Jersey", we get a view of how Coach Bryant himself saw the situation heading into that pivotal 1971 season.

"One-day last week Bryant sat in his office in Tuscaloosa and dissected what had happened. Mostly, he used the scalpel on himself. 'We kind of lost something the last two years. Confidence in ourselves...leadership. I blame myself. I've done a lousy job lately. I guess I got to a point where I just expected things to happen instead of making them happen. People were licking their chops to get at us. Before, well, they weren't real anxious to play us.

He stubbed out his cigarette, lit another one. For a moment he stared at the photographs of his classic teams of the early 1960s that hang on the wall opposite his desk. 'We're starting to get it back now,' he said. He pointed at the photos. 'Confidence is what those teams had and that's what we are rebuilding.'"

The defense was showing some improvement but was still a work in process as he and his staff adapted to the new realities of how the game was being played, and while the offense had established records for yards and points over the last two years, the lack of game control was destructive, and there was frankly no Namath or Stabler to individually lift the level of play.

Alabama needed a schematic edge, something to level the playing field and give the adjustments that Bryant was making on and off the field to take effect. A forced attempt to open the offense and utilize a vertical passing attempt had not succeeded, so the answer lay in returning, at least conceptually, to his roots. Rock-solid defense, an offensive scheme that could control the clock and field position when needed, and an emphasis on discipline, fundamentals, execution, physicality, and the value of quality depth.

The answer lay in the West. The University of Texas, under Bryant's friend Darrel Royal, had debuted a new three-back offense utilizing a heavy dose of triple-option football called the wishbone. They rode it to a couple of national titles, and it was showing up in other places as well, and in the tie in Houston, he and the staff got to see some elements of the offense up close, as Oklahoma had adopted the formation, though they had not, as yet, totally committed to the triple option. The ability to mirror plays, the use of three running backs, and the emphasis on a quarterback who had toughness, great fundamentals, quick hands, and the guts of a burglar instead of just elite arm strength or over-the-top athleticism seemed to play to the strengths of Bryant's spring starter, Terry Davis, and it also allowed him to put together the best rotation of offensive linemen, with the emphasis on the interior three instead of more dominant tackles. Additionally, it was hoped that the offense, as it had at Texas, would take some of the pressure off of the defense as it absorbed the changes in composition, style, and scheme.

It was a bold and courageous choice. Bryant's past success and his impact on almost every aspect of the athletic department in Tuscaloosa would have guaranteed him more time, and quite a bit of leeway, but his own competitive nature and pride provided a harsher judgment. While there was still a lot of talent in Tuscaloosa, and a gifted and veteran staff, perception can sometimes become reality, and the growing concern that the magic had run out on the Capstone could have been fatal to the dreams of a dominant program.

Kirk McNair, whose history and connection with the Alabama football program has no need of being documented, opined in an article he wrote on BamaOnLine.com that "following his second six-win season in 1970, coach Paul Bryant may have been seriously considering retirement. Instead, he resurrected Crimson Tide football. Years later when I asked him what he wanted to be remembered for he said 'Building back Alabama again'".

McNair offers even more proof of his assertion. In the same posting, he relates that he was not the only one who felt that the change to the wishbone and the return to his coaching roots "reinvigorated" the veteran coach, alluding to a conversation he had later with star running back and noted Bryant favorite Johnny Musso. The wishbone, and its inherent return to his game-control style of coaching, would be the key factor over the second half of Bryant's career at Alabama, involving twelve years of his twenty-five-year total. In many ways, it had to be akin to "coming home", and it sparked not only the program to excellence but the coach as well.

As I documented in my previous work, *Crimson Fraternity*, the move to the wishbone involved a CIA-level amount of information control, misdirection, and security, punctuated by the level of access common at the time and the frailties of human nature. From the secreting of Coach Emory Bellard at a local hotel outside the city for meetings with the staff so that they could become instant experts in the elements of the new offense, to the herculean efforts of Kirk McNair and his fellows in sports information to keep local media and the "skywriters", the pool of regional writers who would tour the camps of the major Southern teams to preview their chances in the fall by airplane, to the restrictions and threats of dismissal levied on the players, Bryant sought for both surprise against the vaunted USC Trojans in game one, and for time to get his players and staff acclimated to the new system. With the notable instance of a player who let the cat out of the bag to his local paper, which Bryant papered over by insisting that the Tide had always featured a three-back set for short-yardage and goal-line situations, and the occasional accidental exposure to visitors at practice, whether media or others, the secret stayed safe up until the kickoff in Los Angeles, though one instance, with Bryant's on contrivance, stands out to me. Quoting from *Crimson Fraternity*;

"The most interesting, and I believe illuminating, story about this time and the push to keep the offense a secret, occurred on game week. It was the custom to hold a night practice to accommodate the player's lab schedules, and on this particular evening, the student body of the University decided, unprompted by the administration or Athletics department, to hold a pep rally at Denny Chimes. A large crowd gathered in support of the big game in Los Angeles, and the spirit overflowed to the point where they decided to march to the football practice field and show their ardent spirit to their fellow students in Crimson. When the substantial gathering reached the gates, the staff and players were not only surprised, but in a bit of a panic, afraid their herculean efforts were about to be for naught, but Bryant reacted completely differently. He sent the head manager to open the gate and invite the excited students inside, realizing that most of them would not recognize what they were seeing, and even if a handful did, the risk of that information spreading to anyone who could release it to a wider audience was minimal. Even more importantly, the Coach knew that the enthusiasm and fervor would be a boost for his team, and 'He thought they would like to see what their classmates were doing'". (McNair, interview)

Over the succeeding years, the offense would attract some players, and be a point of consideration for others, but the eventual run of success would speak loudest. During my interviews for both books, it became apparent there were more than a few players who mentioned being swayed by the schemes found elsewhere, but the belief that Bryant would produce winning teams and championships outweighed all other considerations.

Jack White

If honor has a sound, it would much resemble the voice of Mr. Jack White, a swing offensive lineman for the 1971 team at the University of Alabama. I was privileged to spend a part of a lovely afternoon interviewing Jack and it is an exercise that I would highly recommend. Fifty years removed from that season, the pride and competitiveness still ring true, and the lessons he learned, hard-won in the crucible of the proving grounds of Alabama football, still resonate in every word he spoke.

He started his career in Louisville, Mississippi, a linebacker and tight end who caught the eye of Ole Miss, Mississippi State, Southern Miss, and Georgia Tech, but not the school he desired to hear from the most. Jack and his family had lived on the Alabama Gulf Coast, watching *The Bear Bryant Show* and dreaming of a future in Crimson and White. Alabama didn't come calling so after some contemplation and a trip to tour the campus in Oxford, he and his high school friend and teammate Joe decided to accept scholarships to Ole Miss. They both had a fondness for the nearby Mississippi State Bulldogs, but that program was in the midst of some serious struggles. As he recalled, they both agreed that as much as they liked MSU, they wanted to go somewhere they could be part of a winning program.

However, the best-laid plans oft go awry, and this one certainly did. Two days before signing day, the Rebel's staff called to inform Jack that they had offered more scholarships than they had to sign and that his offer was rescinded.

It was a crushing blow. Jack called Joe to tell him the bad news, and his friend reacted as a good friend should, telling him that if he would wait a bit, there would be one coming open soon. A grateful White advised him not to make the call until he contacted Mississippi State and made sure they still had room for him, and when that agreement was consummated, Jack began to search for a new solution.

Unfortunately, his high school coach had informed all the college recruiters that he was signing with the Rebels, and options were scarce. Eventually, Jack accepted a walk-on offer to Mississippi State and went to Jackson to participate in the Mississippi High School All-Star game.

It was in Jackson that his fortunes changed and that his path to Tuscaloosa began to manifest itself. He told me, more than once, that as a born-again Christian, he had a strong belief that many members of the 1971 team, especially those of his senior class, were led to Alabama for a purpose, and his story certainly supports his assertion. In Jackson, as he practiced for the All-Star game, he developed a relationship with Alabama signee David Bailey, a highly-recruited wide receiver. One day, Bailey informed the surprised and disbelieving White that an Alabama coach would be arriving soon to discuss a scholarship offer, and, in due time, Coach Ken Donahue informed the still incredulous Louisville native that he was wanted in Tuscaloosa, though he had had no previous contact and had never visited the campus. The coach revealed that they had been watching him during practice, and felt he was someone who could contribute to the Alabama program. When Coach Donahue asked him if he was willing to come to Tuscaloosa and play for Coach Bryant, the answer was a quick "Yes sir, I can come."

The next question was when could his parents meet with the staff to sign the papers, and after a quick call home, the answer was "We will be there tomorrow." The paper was signed, a quick trip to Tuscaloosa was arranged, and the newest Tide player finally got to see the campus mere weeks before fall camp began.

An addendum to the story, one which both illustrates one of my favorite aspects of writing these books and the true impact of what such decisions can mean to a player and his family. It is my custom to ask, at the end of the interview, if there is a question they have never been asked that they wanted to answer, or if there is something that they wished people knew about them that they didn't. After remarking that what first came to mind was the times he had answered questions that he shouldn't have, he finally related the capper to the recruiting story.

"The first time I ever saw my Dad cry was the time he came to Jackson to sign my scholarship papers. He got out of the car in Jackson and hugged me, and I could see the tears in his eyes."

Jack would end his time in Tuscaloosa in the Spring of 1972, then spend three years on the staff at Alabama before following Jim Sharpe to Virginia Tech as an offensive line coach, installing the wishbone offense and seeing an improvement from 4-7 in the first year to 8-3 the following year, only to be blindsided by the decision of the Athletic Director to forego a Tangerine Bowl invite, a fatal blow to recruiting and creating a new atmosphere in Blacksburg. Eventually, White would leave coaching and spend twenty-five years with the PGA TOUR of America, but admitted to me that when asked by an employee when he stopped missing coaching, the answer was "I'll let you know when it happens". As an old coach myself, I heartily concur. He mentioned that the opportunity to coach good players and good people, and the special brotherhood of coaches, those he worked with and against, were some of the most special privileges of time spent coaching football.

After arriving at Tuscaloosa, it became apparent to Jack that his future was not at linebacker. He was adept at defending the running game and diagnosing plays, but his lack of top-end speed made it almost impossible to cover speedy backs in man coverage. The move to the offensive line soon followed, but once again he found himself at a disadvantage in the pass-happy offense Alabama deployed with Scott Hunter under center.

"The best thing that ever happened to my career was going to the wishbone. I was a pretty good run blocker, but not good at drop-back pass blocking. My lack of size and length was an issue in pass protection and the offense in '69 and '70 had changed from the I-formation and power runs with play action to a pass-first attack with the running game mostly coming from draw plays. The change gave me a chance to play"

The switch to the wishbone, as has been documented in my book Crimson Fraternity and other works, was a well-guarded secret and White had a hand in that operation.

White had gotten married in the Spring of 1971, and the couple moved into the converted barracks near campus. His offseason workouts were planned around his job at the paper mill, and one day he answered a summons to the lower gym to help with something for the upcoming season.

He was greeted by strips of tape on the floor, some quarterbacks and fullbacks, and an oath of secrecy. They needed players to mimic defensive actions so that the quarterbacks could practice the "step-ride-explode" footwork of the fullback exchange in private while reading live bodies. Warned that revealing this to anyone, even his new bride, could result in his exile from the team, Jack was witness to the beginnings of the wishbone transformation.

The information was eventually shared with the rest of the squad in the famous meeting where Bryant informed his players they were switching to the triple-option offense made famous under Darryl Royal at Texas. The veteran coach explained that they were going to "sink or swim" with the new offense, and once again warned them all to keep it secret, giving the team an edge against the powerful Southern Cal

Trojans, who had humbled the Tide in Birmingham the year before.

Along with the change in offense came changes to the offensive line itself. Powerful John Hannah, who would go on to be considered one of the greatest professional offensive linemen of his generation, and Jimmy Rosser, who White identified as the most underrated of the starting linemen, were moved inside to guard, where their ability to solo block defensive tackles and to handle blitzing linebackers became a staple of the Tide's commanding running game that season. Upon hearing the news, Jack immediately asked to be placed at tackle, because with those two at guard the playing time would likely be scarce.

However, Coach Sharpe had a different plan, one harkening to the strategies with which Bryant had begun his tenure in Tuscaloosa. The wily coach had often looked to combine quality depth with outstanding conditioning to allow Alabama to wear down opponents and leave them helpless in the fourth quarter, and White became a part of that strategy. He was the swing player, the versatile backup to both Hannah and Buddy Brown, with those two generally staring the game and playing the first two series, then Jack entering the fray to spell first one of them, and then the other, providing both rest and some variety in skill and technique. This kept the two bigger players fresher in the late stages and provided a quality and game-proven replacement in times of injury or equipment issues.

This type of arrangement was not uncommon in those days, but would probably be more difficult to sell to the modern player. "I was glad to back up Hannah and Brown. I could look at them and see they were starters, but I enjoyed what I did and how it helped the team to be better."

He would make one start that season, in place of an ailing Brown against Miami. When the coach announced his name as a starter, his butterflies calmed when Sharpe quietly told him, "You're ready"

The transition to the new offense, and the re-shaping of the program, the commitment to the standard of play and preparation that Bryant referenced as the path back to the confidence and aura of earlier Tide teams, came about during the most strenuous and difficult spring and summer training session that White ever endured during his time at the Capstone. He recalled a meeting with Bryant at the request of the senior players, in which they voiced their concerns over the attitudes of some of their fellow players. There were those whom the group felt that football did not have the proper significance for, and who were not willing to sacrifice for the good of the team. They were sick of the mediocrity of back-to-back six-win seasons and longed for a return to the harsher environment of previous squads. Bryant's response was brief and ominous. "Look around, some of you won't be here by the season."

It was hard and punishing, but it paid off. Bryant was plain in his intent. If some were going to quit, he intended for it to be on the practice field and not on the playing field. When the real battle began, he needed a weapon tried in the fire and found ready.

The move to the new offense was crucial as well. The wishbone triple-option attack, with its emphasis on execution, repetition, toughness, intelligence, and teamwork, was ready-made for Bryant's style and outlook. White remarked that it "gave us our best chance to win", and confirmed a belief that I have long held that a major component of the decision was an effort to lighten the load on the beleaguered Tide defense, which had seen its performances deteriorate rapidly during the last two years.

"You can win in the wishbone with less talent than in conventional offenses because you don't block two defenders almost every play. One player is read for the fullback dive and one for the keep-pitch decision, so you have an advantage. If they made a mistake, we had a big advantage. It also allowed us to control the clock. Against Auburn that year, we had around forty minutes of possession, leaving them with only fewer possessions, and we just wore them down in the second half and kept

Sullivan and Beasley off the field. A good wishbone team helps the defense because it keeps them fresh, which makes them aggressive. It was a lot of the same players, except for the linebackers, but it was a much better defense in 1971."

The 1971 season was special in many ways, and when asked about the games that stood out the most in his memory, Jack mentioned several.

"Of course, everyone always points to the USC game, and it was a big win. Trojan coach John McKay would admit that Alabama's switch to a full wishbone offense did catch him off guard, but it was the fact that the defense that had given up forty-two points the year before held them to ten that made the big difference. To me, the Ole Miss, Mississippi State, and Southern Miss games were important, being from Mississippi and playing against guys I knew, but the one that stands out the most, the one that had the whole team jacked up, was the Tennessee game. They had shut us out the year before, that hadn't happened to Coach Bryant for a long time and we were the ones who let it happen. We were so physical in that game, the most physical game of my whole career. No one who played let up at all, it was full bore. They had a linebacker who had done a lot of talking the year before, talking trash and rubbing it in our faces. I can tell you we wanted to make sure he remembered this game. Nothing illegal or cheap, but we looked him up a lot and made sure he did remember it. That game helped us to re-establish ourselves by dominating them."

Bryant had come into the season looking to return the Crimson Tide to dominance, to make them once again a team other teams dreaded to play. After the convincing 32-15 win over the Volunteers, the aura had returned. When asked if the "Bear was back?", Tennessee head coach and former Bama player Bill Battle responded with visible surprise in the Pat Putnam article, "I didn't realize he had gone anywhere. He's just back to coaching his kind of game--jaw-to-jaw, hard-nosed football. And now he has the players for it."

As for the Auburn game that season, there were two things that sprang to mind for Mr. White. The first, which he felt had some significant impact on the mentality of the team, was the knowledge the team had about their bowl destination and the matchup that awaited them. It was already decided, even before Oklahoma and Nebraska played two days before the game in Birmingham, that Alabama would be traveling to Miami to face the Cornhuskers in the Orange Bowl, while Auburn would head to New Orleans for a date with the Sooners in the Sugar Bowl. Based on the outcomes of the two games in November, two of the teams would have a shot at the national championship, the dream that had driven White and his teammates all season.

After watching Nebraska win a thrilling 35-31 contest which has been dubbed "the game of the century" (one of many to be so titled, but that is the way of the world) Jack felt that his team got a mental boost by knowing that, if they won in Birmingham, they would face the Cornhuskers straight up for the national title. To his mind, the result was already determined. The Tigers would not stand in the way of the dream, not after all the hard work and sacrifice. He related to me something Coach Bryant said to them about what separated the Crimson Tide from many of their opponents. "Over there in that other locker room, they are sitting and thinking about how great it would be to beat us, but we were sitting there thinking about how bad we were going to beat them."

The other memory came at halftime of the game itself. Alabama had played well, corralling the dangerous Sullivan and Beasley and forging a 14-7 lead with the only Tiger touchdown coming off a halfback pass from Harry Unger. However, they had seen Sullivan, three years in a row, find a way to rally his team to victory and the thought was lingering for some. Former roommate Jeff Beard, as they walked off the field headed for the locker, looked at the scoreboard and wondered out loud if they weren't just being set up for another comeback heartbreaker. White had a different vision.

"They are done. You want to know why? Because you and Rowell are going to be all over Sullivan, they can't run on us, and we are going to grind them down on offense." The response was brief but meaningful. "Oh, yeah".

And, they did just that. During the conversation, White was able to answer a question that I had pondered for many years about how the defense was able to control the potent Tiger passing attack and be in the right place so often. Apparently, it was something Oliver and the defensive staff had picked up in film study and scouting. "If Sullivan was going to throw to his left, he took the snap and backpedaled, but if he was going to look to his right, he used a more common turn-and-drop technique. This allowed the defense to rotate to that side, and cut off a lot of their timing routes." It was simple, but effective, and took some guts to commit to, but along with the fierce pass rush of Parkhouse and Rowell and Mitchell and Beard, it worked to almost perfection."

Mr. White, as we conversed that day, agreed with me that there was, and still is, something special about this group of men. They remain close to this day, any meeting of any of them taking on the nature of a briefly interrupted conversation, many of them sharing a bond not only of memories and victories but of a shared faith that deepened an already profound connection. "That whole season, the transition, the hard work and sacrifice, our confidence and mentality just got stronger and stronger. Coach Bryant would tell us that the other team was going to come out on the field with tears in their eyes and snot-bubbles blowing, but if we would just line up and knock them on their ___ play after play, the tears would dry up and the bubbles would pop and the best team would win. And, he was right."

One last story, because it gives great insight to the man and the team and the cost of success. And, because I could not bear to leave it out. Walking off the field after the last practice in Tuscaloosa before they were to head to Miami for the bowl game, White was talking with defensive end Robin Parkhouse and mentioned how lucky they were to have been a part of it all. Parkhouse looked around and replied, "I wouldn't take a million dollars for this experience, but I wouldn't do it again for a million dollars either." I would imagine that is a sentiment not unique to the two of them, that mixture of humor and shared burden, but I also know that the memories and the bonds that were forged in that crucible last untarnished today.

The First Quarter

The Auburn Tigers started the 1971 season with high hopes and great expectations. Coming off of a 9-2 season that featured a come from behind victory over Alabama and a solid victory over Tennessee with a bowl victory over Ole Miss in the Gator Bowl, and with an offense built around Sullivan and Beasley and experience on the defense, the Tigers roared out of the gate with a blow-out of an overmatched Chattanooga and throttling of Kentucky sandwiched around a thrilling 10-9 victory over Tennessee in Knoxville, in which the Tigers overcame a couple of turnovers, one after a long drive in the fourth quarter at the Volunteer's goal line. Sullivan was cool, calm, and courageous, and Beasley was magnificent. The defense made the plays they had to, and the 2-0 conference record put the Tigers right where they wanted to be, in prime contention for a conference title and a number four AP ranking. All the chips were on the table, and Sullivan was already on the national radar. The way the season was beginning to play out, Tennessee looked to be the biggest threat to the Tiger's hopes until they faced the gauntlet of Mississippi State, Georgia, and possibly Alabama to end the year.

Alabama, on the other hand, was a bit of a wildcard entering the year. They faced the task of replacing a record-setting starting quarterback, repairing a leaking defense, and reestablishing their alpha status in the region. Coming off back to back six-win seasons, and facing a USC team that had completely dominated them in Birmingham the previous year, the Tide returned the visit to Los Angeles and shocked the Trojans and the nation with a 17-10 victory over the heavily favored Californians, unveiling the wishbone and following the running of Musso and company, the physical nature of the offensive line, and the option wizardry of Davis to an early 17-0 lead, and then depending on ball control and defense to finish the job.

The Tide followed up this outcome with dominant results over Southern Miss at home and Florida in Gainesville. Alabama was the better team, but the fact that they were able to play that way in the early stages of a new offense that had only been in existence for about seven weeks was promising. Additionally, the defense showed signs of returning to the Alabama standard, and the Crimson Tide soared to number seven in the rankings preparatory to a showdown with Ole Miss in Birmingham in week four.

The first quarter of the Iron Bowl would feature some of the best characteristics of the beginning of the season for Alabama, and some diametrically opposite results for the Tigers. Alabama would explode out of the gate with early success, while Sullivan and the Tigers would stumble and bumble, with turnovers and mistakes placing them in an early hole.

Auburn won the opening toss and elected to receive, as always placing their trust in Sullivan, Beasley and their prolific offense. Greg Gant's kick off hit at the ten-yard line and bounced over the head of the returner, and into the end zone, giving the Tigers the ball at the twenty.

Two early runs produced a grand total of three yards, setting the tone for the day, and Sullivan retreated to pass for the first time, hitting Lowry on a swing route in the left flats. Cornerback Steve Williams made the first of several big plays for the Crimson Tide defensive unit, with a sure tackle that stopped the Tiger halfback a yard short of the first down, and set up the first key play of the game.

Auburn punter David Beverly was unable to cleanly field the low, bouncing snap, and was subsequently smothered by big John Mitchell at the Tiger twenty, providing Davis and the offense with tremendous field position. The Tide did not waste it, as on third-and-eight after two ineffective running plays, Davis, on the counter option, which will prove to be a key weapon in the first half, ripped off a gain of ten behind a key block from fullback Steve Bisceglia. Then, on a second and goal from the six, Davis again found daylight on the counter option, dashing for paydirt and putting the Tide up 7-0 after a successful Bill Davis PAT. Less than five minutes into the 1971 Iron Bowl, Alabama had gained a significant advantage, as the wishbone was especially adept at playing with a lead.

After Henley returned the kickoff out to the Tiger twenty-seven, Auburn began their second possession with a return to their bread-and-butter, a quick slant to Beasley for seven yards. Another textbook tackle by Williams kept it from gaining more, but, after narrowly avoiding what appeared to be a sure sack, Sullivan hit the reliable Schmalz for sixteen down the center of the Alabama coverage, providing the Tiger faithful signs of life and setting up the offense at the midfield stripe.

However, the surge would ebb again. A run for no gain and a quick slant to Beasley for five set up a third-and-five, and once again it was Sullivan to Beasley, and once again, Steve Williams showed his true metal, with another outstanding open-field stop that yet again left Auburn one yard short of the marker. Jordan called for a punt, and this time Beverley successfully got it off, but it meandered its way into the endzone, giving Davis and his wishbone mates possession at their own twenty.

The eighty yards that lay between Alabama and the promised land were navigated with an impressive array of skills, featuring Musso, Davis, LaBue, and their fellows doing what they did best. Musso, shrugging off the pain and limitations of his injury, converted a third-and-four with the pitch on the valuable counter option play, using a well-executed block from LaBue and a hurdle of the first defender, then finishing with a dive over two more Tigers. Davis, after a shift to an I-formation and three wideouts, completes his first pass attempt of the day, hitting LaBue in the flats and watching the underrated halfback sprint for sixteen yards.

LaBue continued his contributions, racing for seven yards on a crossbuck carry, then hitting another key block on the triple option pitch to Musso to spring him for sixteen yards. Then, one play later, it was Davis again on the counter option, with huge blocks from Bisceglia and Musso eliminating defenders, and Terry sprinting through a desperation arm tackle on his way to the endzone. Another made extra point, and it was 14-0 Tide, and the momentum was absolutely Crimson.

Auburn, after a fine Staggers return to the thirty, found five yards for Unger on a crossbuck, and then, on the final play of the opening quarter, tried their first trick play, a reverse to Beasley that briefly looked promising, but ended with lost yardage when a stout effort by that man Williams again forced the wideout to cut sharply and to lose his footing and fall to the turf of Legion Field.

With the clock showing zeros after the first fifteen minutes of action, Alabama had dominated play and owned a 14-0 lead. Sullivan had gotten the ball into Beasley's hand several times, but the mercurial wideout had been held in check, and the Tigers had almost no success running the ball.

Alabama, on the other hand, had moved the ball effectively, especially using misdirection, and the stellar play of Williams on the right flank of the defense had led to two key stops and prevented two other plays from becoming bigger gains. The pace and the scoreboard certainly favored the Tide, but memories of last year's debacle when a similar 17-0 lead had evaporated under the brilliance of Sullivan and Beasley flitted through more than one Crimson memory.

Now, the change back to more game and clock control would be put to the test.

Lanny Norris

Romans 8:28 says the following: "And we know that all things work together for good to them that love God, to them who are called according to his purpose." Lanny Norris, a former defensive back at the University of Alabama and highly successful businessman in his home region quoted that verse to me during our interview, and I can think of no more appropriate introduction to the man for readers than that. It encapsulates the man, his philosophy, and much of his story as he related it to me on a bitterly cold night in January, and its promise has certainly been realized in his life.

I do most of these interviews sitting at our dining room table, with my legal pad and the phone on speaker so that I can take notes and occasionally look up facts or numbers, and while my wife is usually ensconced in our bedroom, about as far away from my station as possible. Sometimes, he sometimes wanders through, and can, with the door open, hear parts of the conversation. After talking with Mr. Norris, I walked into our bedroom to find her sitting on the bed, beaming from ear to ear. In response to my curious expression, she told me, "It just amazes me how many of these guys share their strong Christian faith with you and how much it is a part of their lives. It is a recurrent thread in so many of your interviews." And, she is absolutely right. I am impressed again and again by the bonds that still strongly unite these players from those early 70s teams, and a powerful element of that is a shared Faith and a family paradigm.

Lanny's story is interwoven with his faith and his commitment to the concept of using his talents and success to make not only those around him, family, coaches, teammates, and others proud of him, but participants in that success.

"Coach Bryant always told us he wanted us to play and act so that our Momma and Daddy and our high school coaches would be proud of us while we were there. Success is not just about you, but so that they could enjoy it too. I was very fortunate in the coaches I played for and worked with. Even in 7th grade, I played on the first junior high team at Russellville and had a wonderful guy, then on to high school for Coach Doty and his staff, then Coach Bryant, Coach Moore, and Coach Oliver at Alabama and working for Coach Dye at East Carolina. And, I was blessed with good parents, great siblings, two brothers who I wanted to be like, and my sister. As the youngest of the four, they were who I looked up to. Later, when I was trying to please my coaches I was still trying to make my Dad and my brothers proud of how I played."

The road to becoming the starting strong safety in Tuscaloosa was one of the surprising twists and fortunate events for Norris. Coach Doty, who was a legend in North Alabama and a coach that I greatly respected during my career, built a juggernaut in Russelville, and garnered state championships during the era of voted champions, including the team Norris played on as a junior. Then, in his senior season when the switch was made to a playoff system, the Golden Tigers made a championship run with Lanny playing quarterback and defensive back, which attracted attention to both the program and its best players. Norris was a star on both sides, though he professed to a preference for defense, but was unsure of whether any college was eager to sign a 6'1'' 160lb defensive back.

"Coach Doty was old-school, didn't want us knowing if we were being looked at. Sometimes word would get out, but he never said anything. I didn't know Alabama had any interest in me, even though Coach Rutledge was around some and I saw him. We were playing for a championship, in the early stages of a long winning streak, and I didn't realize that he was there looking at me.

I was sitting in Mrs. Goggan's English class in December when the principal called me to the office. I went, wondering what I had done wrong and if I was in trouble. Coach introduced me to a man who stood up and told me he was a graduate assistant at Alabama and that Coach Bryant had sent him to offer me a scholarship. My jaw hit the floor. It didn't take long to say yes. I loved Alabama, loved Coach Bryant and now I had the chance to play for him."

There was more to the story that Norris did not learn of until later on. Coach Rutledge had been impressed but had not made the final report to Bryant due to his hectic schedule, so the head coach had not seen the film cutups showcasing Lanny's talents. Coach Doty, convinced his safety was good enough to play at Alabama, made a call, and Coach Bryant watched the film on his own, then quickly dispatched a man to make the offer.

"The SEC limited teams to 45 players in a class, and I like to tell people that I was probably the 45th guy in my class. We didn't have a weight program at Russellville, even with all our success, and I knew I had some ground to make up, but I felt like I was a good player and I was determined to play, to do whatever it took to get good enough to wear that jersey."

However, the journey would not be without its pitfalls. A freak accident not long before he was to report resulted in a trip to Tuscaloosa to see Jim Goostree, the team trainer, and a quick diagnosis of a torn meniscus. The ensuing surgery wiped out his freshman fall, but freshmen were ineligible for varsity play so it was a time of recovery and learning, with an interesting and formative end result when spring training came around.

"Mike Dean was the starter at strong safety, my position, and he was a senior. He came to Coach Bryant and asked if he could play baseball that spring, so when Coach posted the roster and schedule for spring practice, I was down as the starting strong safety. Mike was not there and I had some experience in terms of learning the position and technique, so I got most of the reps.

After the first week of Spring, Coach Bryant put out the training table list. This meant you ate in the smaller dining hall, and that you got steak every night. It was something you earned, and I had had a good week. There were only two freshmen on that list, me and Musso, so I felt like I was in really good company."

The story continues, as do the twists and turns of life. After a highly successful spring, Norris knew that the returning Dean would be the starter in the fall, but expected to be in the mix for significant playing time given that experience. Roughly a week before the opening game against Virginia Tech, on a toss play to Musso in practice, things changed again.

" I came up to make the tackle, and Musso put one of his moves on me. All I had left was to throw out my arm and try to grab him, but my arm got caught between him and our middle linebacker, and it broke completely. And, that was the end of my season that year."

Though he admitted to some discouragement in missing the first two falls of his college career, it was at this point that Lanny quoted the passage from Romans to me, and explained why he thought it applied.

"It seemed like a bad turn at the time, but I traded that 1969 season, which was a really tough year, a 6-5 season, for an extra year in 1972 as a redshirt. I was able to get my masters, play on an undefeated team that played for a national championship, and got the opportunity to play on a very good team in '72. And the real prize was that I met my wife in 1972 at a Bible study class. I had seen her before but never met her. I tell people it was love at first sight for me, but it took a little longer for her."

This attitude, this philosophy of life, recurred during our talk. Lanny Norris believes in the message of Romans 8:28 and with good reason. He has seen the evidence.

1970 would also be, by Alabama standards, a difficult season, but Norris points to the building blocks that would become the foundation for the future success that would begin in 1971. As much as it is common to point to the implementation of the wishbone offense as a key to the resurgence of the Crimson Tide program, as we have pointed out elsewhere, it was the return to dominance on defense, aided by the ball control and scoring efficiency of the wishbone, that led to the multiple championship contenders wearing Crimson in the next few years.

As with all such transitions, there are several contributing factors and Lanny pointed them out to me.

"We added a few good players between 1970 and 1971, including a couple of junior college guys who had experience, but mostly, we just got older and bigger and stronger. I got to 192 myself, all muscle on our lifting and eating program, and the changes we made in our scheme began to pay off when we got older and smarter."

There were, as there always are, some bumps in the road, but even those contributed to learning and experience.

"Before the 1970 season, Coach Mal Moore, who was still working with the defense at that point, went out to watch the Dallas Cowboys and the things they were doing. They had switched to a mostly man-coverage scheme for pass defense in response to the way Joe Namath had picked apart the zone defenses of the Colts in the Super Bowl. Coach Moore changed us to a more man concept, not abandoning our zone coverages but playing more man. Now, man coverage is great if you can match the speed and talent of the offense, but that was an issue for us that year. We started off the season against USC in Birmingham, and of course, you know we got beat soundly and everyone remembers Cunningham running all over us, but the thing I remember is lining up over the slot receiver and trying to run with him and getting beat deep two or three times. Fortunately, the quarterback missed the throw, but they had three really great athletes at receiver and we just couldn't match up with them.

At the end of the season, Coach Moore went over to coach the quarterbacks and Coach Bryant brought in Bill "Brother" Oliver to coach the defensive backs. He returned us to a more zone-oriented system, but we learned some things running all that man. The thing Coach Oliver brought to us was his belief that execution was more important than scheme."

Moore would find a more comfortable fit on offense, but it was a trait he shared with Oliver, one that would carry over from 1970 to 1971, that would pay off handsomely against the Auburn Tigers in Legion Field.

"For me, our success in '71 against Auburn went back to that 1970 season. We had two weeks to prepare for them like we did every year, and Coach Moore, as he did, pored over every inch of film. He realized that Sullivan was giving away which side he was passing to by the way he did his drop. If he turned his shoulders and dropped, he was throwing to the right, and if he back peddled, he was going left. Eleven game films, he did it every single time. Also, they ran a lot of what we called complementary routes, using two receivers on either side. If you read the release of the inner receiver, the tight end, or the slot, you had a good idea what the other route would be. And, of course, he was right."

Unfortunately, all of this knowledge would go out the window by the second half of that memorable, or painful depending on your point of view, comeback Tiger win. It started at the beginning of the two weeks of preparation when starting corner Steve Williams, who would be a key performer in the '71 contest, was injured in a freakish off-field accident. His replacement Bobby McKinney was not as experienced or accomplished, but at least they had the time to get him ready to read the routes quickly and make the necessary adjustments, and by kickoff, he was up-to-speed, at the cost of getting almost all the practice reps. The first half went gloriously for the Tide, sprinting out to a commanding lead behind the impressive running of Musso and the utilization of Coach Moore's scouting to shut down the explosive Sullivan-Beasley combination.

Then, as often happens in competitive sports, everything changed in a matter of a few moments of game time. After a long Musso run put the Tide in scoring position again near the end of the first half, a Tiger interception in the endzone, and the resultant return gave them new life and the ball near mid-field. A score just before the half made it 21-7 and things went even more downhill in the second half.

"Bobby was running on a go route with Beasley, step for step, then he pulls his hamstring. I was on the move to help, but he couldn't keep up and though he did hold on enough to make the tackle, the long completion gave them great field position. Even worse than giving up another score was losing Bobby because the guys behind him just didn't have any experience and had gotten hardly any reps since he needed the extra work."

Sullivan, sensing blood in the water, went to work on the inexperienced replacements, and the quick-strike Auburn attack was in full effect. Norris told me that at one point, he considered asking Coach Bryant to move him to corner since he knew the reads and techniques, but "I was just a sophomore and didn't think it was my place."

The next year, with the return to a more complimentary pass coverage scheme, and the play of defense overall, things would be vastly different.

"We had two great defensive ends, Robin Parkhouse and John Mitchell, and two very good defensive tackles, though they were opposites physically. Jeff Beard had that typical thick lineman body, but his partner Terry Rowell, who had been a great high school running back in Mississippi, was about 195lbs, he was really quick and athletic and the offensive linemen had a real hard time trying to block him.

At linebacker, we had Tom Surlas, who like Mitchell came to us from a junior college, and Jeff Rouzie, who would have been a consensus All-American the next year if he hadn't been involved in a serious car accident that ended his career, and Chuck Strickland.

In the secondary, you had the three Steves. Higginbotham, Williams, and Wade along with me.

We were a very seasoned defense and we were better physically. Just smarter and better, the scheme fit us, and with the keys Coach Moore gave us, which Auburn hadn't changed at all, we shut them down pretty good. The final score, 31-7, looks like a blowout, but it was a seven or ten-point game into the fourth quarter. I really think if we hadn't lost Steve and Bobby, it would have been two wins instead of one."

When asked about his memories of that '71 season, there were a handful of games outside of the Auburn contest, and yet another example of adversity leading to success. Let's take the games first.

"Obviously, beating USC was big. We played a lot of good teams, including Nebraska at the end, but I don't think anyone had any more talent than USC, so beating them, especially after the season before, meant a lot.

The Tennessee game comes to mind. We hadn't beaten them since maybe 1967, and we took it to them in Legion Field. The Ole Miss game had taken on a bit of a rivalry feel, and we handled them pretty good in Birmingham too.

Defensively, you may be surprised by this, but one of the toughest games that year was Houston. They had Robert

Newhouse, who went on to a great pro career at Dallas and was built like a fireplug, these big powerful thighs, and Riley Odoms who played with the Broncos, and their quarterback was an excellent athlete as well. I spent a lot of the day trying to tackle Newhouse and he was a load. We had played them the year before in Houston and beat them worse in '71, but they were tough and the crowd wasn't happy because we didn't beat the point spread."

For all the on-field success and the euphoria associated with playing for an undefeated championship contender, Norris once again experienced some personal adversity.

"I had played almost every down as a sophomore. Coming into my junior year, I was in the best shape of my life. I went back home a week before the start of practice, went over to Russellville High School to do some running, and on the last lap, I was feeling so good and running so fast that I pushed it really hard to finish. My hamstring popped and there I was a week before practice, couldn't run, couldn't do anything.

I was in the training room every day leading up to the USC game. David McMakin, a sophomore was my backup and he got all the reps. I finally got well enough to practice a week before we went to California. I wasn't fully ready, so

David started, and I came in later and played about half the game. For the first four or five games, we split it about 50/50. David would go on to start on the '73 championship team, and by the second half of the season, I was playing well."

After finishing the 1972 season, Norris was eager to try coaching. He approached Coach Bryant about getting into coaching, feeling after five years he had a good grasp of the fundamentals of playing the game, and in a matter of a few days, Bryant called him to his office to tell Lanny that he had spoken to Frank Broyles at Arkansas, who had a similar situation with a former player, and so the two veteran coaches made an unofficial "swap". After a fall in Fayetteville, Norris received a call from Coach Pat Dye, who had been the linebacker coach at Alabama during his time there, with an invitation to join him at East Carolina University, where Dye had just procured his first head coaching job. This would lead to three years in Greenville, North Carolina, coaching the defensive backs and starting a new life with his new bride.

"I went in January of 1974, then came back in June of that year and got married. My wife was an elementary school teacher, and she got a job teaching second grade. To tell you how different times were, she made more money than I did."

Four years of coaching led to many great memories, a relationship with Coach Dye, and the special connection that the best coaches create with their players, but the arrival of a daughter led to a period of evaluation when he realized that he had barely seen her during her first weeks and months of life because he was in the midst of the season. The decision was made to return to Alabama and seek a different career, a move that led to a long and distinguished career in the insurance field.

"Why did I quit coaching? I like to tell people it's because I had a vision; a vision that said if I had stayed three more years I would have had to have gone with Coach Dye to Auburn. Couldn't do that."

It's a good story for a laugh, but both of us understood. He mentioned the advice that Coach Bryant gave to a lot of young coaches, to the effect that if you can imagine living doing anything else, coaching is probably not the career for you. Like Lanny, one day I looked at my family and decided that the joys of coaching were not worth the time away from my family, and walked away, so I understand exactly what brought him back to Alabama and his life here.

When we concluded our conversation, as I have with all the others, discussing the way that Coach Bryant had of creating a desire to please him and seek his approval, and of what he would like his career to be remembered for, Norris returned to the themes of family, shared success and pride.

"Coach Bryant was just a commanding presence. He was a big man, and that was some of it, but he had the presence and the reputation, and when you met him he was a living legend. When we had a team meeting, the players would be sitting in the room, talking and being young men, and the other coaches would gather at the door, but when he came in, no one had to tell you to get quiet, sit up, and pay attention. You just did it. It was like the old E.F. Hutton commercials, where the tag line was 'when E.F. Hutton speaks, everyone listens.'

You were fearful, but you wanted to do whatever you had to to get his approval. I busted my tail on the practice field because I wanted him to mention me in the meeting the next day. When he did his show, I wanted him to call my name. You feared him, but you loved him. When we played, we didn't care who was in the stands or at the game, we wanted his approval."

I came to realize that wanting his approval, or Coach Doty's or Coach Moore's or all the others, was an extension of wanting my family to be proud of me, of doing something we could all enjoy and be proud of. In trying to please them, I was trying to please my Dad and my brothers who showed me the way."

Today, Lanny Norris can look back on a storied career in both high school and at Alabama, a relationship with some truly extraordinary men, and memories that are rare and precious. But, most of all, he can rest assured that he lived and played and worked in a way that his family, friends, and teammates can always be proud of him, and for him. And, that is a blessing indeed.

Supporting Casts

No football team is a one-man operation. As talented and accomplished as Musso and Sullivan were, their greatest value was in the opportunities they presented to their teammates, and success depended on those players taking advantage of such opportunities. We will look at the respective defenses in another chapter, but to grasp the 1971 Iron Bowl, and the seasons in general, it is important to look at the "supporting casts" on each team.

For Auburn, this starts with a player who just as easily could have been the primary star, wide receiver Terry Beasley. As talented and accomplished as Sullivan was as a quarterback, Beasley's freakishly strong hands, excellent body control, and "burst", not to mention his almost psychic link to Sullivan under pressure, gave the Auburn signal-caller an edge that was almost impossible to counter. Beasley was strong and his above-average speed helped him to gain separation, but it was his advanced route running for the day and ability to use that core strength and powerful hands to "post up" defenders and catch the ball in traffic that made him special. Then, utilizing his exceptional balance and that "burst" he could take an eight-yard catch and turn it into a bigger gain. He was incredible in what is now referred to as the red zone, and his records for career receiving yards, career receiving touchdowns, and season touchdown catches still stand today.

Sadly, his greatness has come with a cost. One of his hallmark attributes was his toughness, catching passes in the crowded areas between linebackers and safeties. This resulted in a lot of contact, often high to his head and neck area, and due to the mores of the day, his own inherent ethic, and his psychological impact on his teammates and the Tiger fanbase, which was second only to Sullivan, if that, he suffered several concussions. There are a couple of famous game action pictures which show a barely conscious, obviously concussed Beasley lying on the field or being revived on the sidelines during critical games that he returned to play in. Though his NFL career lasted only three years due to accumulated injuries, he continued to make highly contested catches in heavy traffic and accumulate more head contact, and today suffers many health issues which can be traced back to the cumulative effects of the concussions. It is a bitter by-product of the combination of the changing nature of the game which included the controlled passing game that resulted in so many more catches in the interior of the defense, where more defenders could contact the receiver and from a bewildering number of angles, bigger, stronger, faster players, and the lag in equipment, especially helmets better suited to the more violent collisions which were focused more and more on the upper torso and head area. Beasley is a victim of his own competitiveness and the failures of the game to adjust to its own evolution.

During the 1970 and 1971 seasons, Beasley was simply the best receiver in the SEC, and arguably the nation. He made the very good Sullivan play like an elite quarterback, and he would have been as worthy a recipient of the Heisman as Sullivan was. His dominant performances against Tennessee and Georgia were keys to those victories, and handling him would be a key to Alabama's hopes.

But, the Tigers and their prolific offense was not just a function of their two superstars. The Auburn attack featured three quality running backs, none of whom had the overall skills and numbers of Musso, but as a threesome, they were highly effective and well-suited for the scheme. Terry Lowrey, Harry Unger, and Terry Henley would combine for around 1200 yards on the ground, contributed in the passing game with short routes and screens, and were all effective blockers in both the running and passing games. They also contributed around fifty catches, and even a pass attempt or two. The offense, built around Sullivan and Beasley, was not built to feature a dominant back, and the skills and talents of the three were blended masterfully.

And then, there were the other two main cogs of the passing attack. Dick Schmalz, the "other end" and TE Robby Robinette took full advantage of the needs for defenses to tilt towards Beasley, and to account for Sullivan's abilities in the open field if the play broke down. Schmalz, while never accumulating huge numbers, was known for big catches at key times, and Robinett figured in a handful of big plays as well.

Of course, no offense is successful without at least good offensive line play, and the Tigers, though a tad undersized, were nimble and well-adapted for the quick passing game, the trap-and-perimeter running game, and the, for the day, extensive screen game that was the primary components of the Auburn attack. They were effective in double teams and played hard for four quarters, which figured into the Tiger's penchant for exciting finishes. However, they were prone to being overpowered by bigger, more physical defenses, and had struggled with Tennessee, which had a defense more similar to the Tide than most of the teams they had faced in 1971. It would be one of the key elements of the game, the matchup of the Tiger O-line and the 'Bama front seven.

On the Alabama side of the equation, it starts with Terry Davis. Davis, as I chronicled in *Crimson Fraternity*, was a coveted high school recruit out of Louisiana who was a prime example of a player whose whole far exceeded his parts. Athletic, fiery, very productive in high school in an offense featuring some option, rollout, and bootleg schemes which allowed him to play in space where his quickness and decision-making were at a premium and his accuracy as a passer was optimized. Early in his tenure in Tuscaloosa, there were attempts to utilize his athleticism on defense, a tactic Bryant would utilize quite often in the 70s.

During the spring before the 1971 season, Davis turned back the challenges of those a bit more suited to continuing the offense run by Hunter, and his decisive leadership and competitive nature, as well as his fundamental grasp of playing quarterback, established him as the starter and contributed to Bryant's decision to move to the wishbone. The triple-option puts a high demand on the quarterback both mentally and physically, since almost every play relies on his ability to read the defense and choose the best option for success, and exposes him to contact on practically every snap Throw in the need for the quarterback to be an effective runner if the defense decides he is the better choice, and the premium on throwing the ball from unconventional launch points and without advanced pass protection schemes and the demands, as I covered in my earlier work, are substantial. Additionally, in the era when quarterbacks still called a majority of the plays on the field, the wishbone quarterback had to be able to decipher the manner in which the defense was trying to attack the scheme and select the proper plays to take advantage.

Davis excelled in the offense. Playing two years in the triple option, Davis would execute and lead at such a rate that he would be selected as quarterback of more than one generational All-SEC and All-Southern team over players with much higher rushing and passing numbers and creditable NFL careers. In my earlier work, I referred to him as "the Engine" and if you care to watch the available film of the period, or if you talk to those who were involved in the program, the name fits. He might not have been the most talented player in any configuration he played in, but he was the key to the offense and the heartbeat of the team.

Putnam in *Sports Illustrated* once again gives us "real-time" evidence from that year.

"Almost from the beginning, Quarterback Terry Davis. A 173-pound junior, took to the triple option as though he had been commanding one all his life. He is not fast, but he has quick feet and he thrives on running. 'We're going to win with him because everybody has confidence in him,' said Musso. Davis will never be a great passer, but he can throw short well enough to keep the defense alert, and that is all Bryant expects.'

He also had a pattern of outplaying opposing star quarterbacks. The two biggest examples, although not the only ones, being this Iron Bowl when, though the offenses were radically different, he completely outplayed the Heisman trophy winner Sullivan, and in 1972 when his domination of the field against LSU and their Heisman hopeful Bert Jones ended the Tigers championship dreams and Jones' campaign in one magical afternoon. Within the dynamic of the wishbone, the combination of Davis and Musso created real issues for defensive coordinators, issues which would eventually overwhelm the Tigers in Birmingham.

Ellis Beck, Steve Bisceglia, Joe LaBue, and Wilbur Jackson, the other inhabitants of the Crimson Tide backfield, were all significant contributors during the season. Statistically, there was a real divide between Musso and his mates, but the three-back arrangement of the wishbone, and Bryant's love of depth and wearing down an opponent, meant that the carries were divided and the load was shared. All four backs averaged over five yards a carry, which is at the very good to elite level, and LaBue was over six. Additionally, all of them, in particular LaBue, were accomplished and selfless blockers and combined with what became a notable offensive line group, allowed the Tide to control the line of scrimmage in most games and to run the ball at want instead of at need. They ran with power, speed, and consistency and, as at Auburn, played off the headliners with efficiency when the opportunity offered.

While the wishbone is not considered a good passing offense, by the end of the decade Alabama would develop an efficient and, at times, deadly passing game by utilizing the athleticism of its running backs and the ability to play versatile athletes at the tight end position along with more developed pass protection concepts. But, in the first few years, all of this was still in the developmental process, and while Davis, and his successor Gary Rutledge, were accurate passers, the passing game did not produce the numbers it would later. This was not the fault of the talent at wide receiver, however, since both David Bailey, who would be lead in catches with 21, and Wayne Wheeler, who would average almost 24 yards a reception, were both good college wideouts and effective in the opportunities they were accorded. However, as many of their coaches and teammates have observed over the years, the biggest contribution to the success of the 1971 Alabama team they made was the graceful, team-first adaptation to the offense in becoming very good perimeter blockers who accepted the fact that fewer balls would be coming their way. Getting talented and acclaimed players to accept reduced personal glory for the sake of stronger team dynamics was always a key benchmark for Bryant and his success, and the wideouts in '71 were prime examples.

Finally, and nearest and dearest to my heart, the offensive line. Buddy Brown, Jimmy Grammer, John Hannah, Jim Krapf, and Jimmy Rosser became a dominant group throughout the season, and while obviously, Hannah would go on to exalted status in the NFL, it was the ability of these five guys along with swingman Jack White, to not only execute the different and sometimes counterintuitive blocking techniques of the triple option but to adapt and adjust together to the unusual and sometimes unique counters to the offense they saw on Saturdays that paved the way for the Tide to roll. The key to defeating the triple option has always been centered on quick penetration to disrupt the quarterback-fullback exchange, and then confusing the reads and blocking assignments on the perimeter, and in the early days of the offense, there were a plethora of means and methods which had to be accounted for. Many of these were faulty, and actually made the offense easier to run, but the sheer amount of different schemes and the fact that Alabama would have little to no film of their opponents running such concepts against other teams, since the wishbone, in the early days, was not widespread, made preparation difficult and in-game adjustments critical. Given the relatively small area that offensive linemen work in and the closeness of the opposition, decisions are made in fractions of a second and in an option offense, require five eyes to see the same things and five minds to make the same evaluations. As you watch the surviving video of the season, you can see the growth and development by the time the Iron Bowl rolled around. Throw in the physical ability of the individual players, the leadership of older players who were tired of losing and willing to pay the price Bryant required to regain the glory of Alabama football, and a relentless work ethic, and the offensive line reached elite status by the end of the season. And, their ability to control the line of scrimmage would indeed be a fundamental element of what occurred in the Old Gray Lady that day.

John Hannah

"I remember as a young fella, going places with my dad, to the barbershop or whatever, and people would ask me because I was a big kid, 'Hey John, you going to be a pro football player like your daddy?' and I would answer them, 'Yes, sir'"

If you know anything about football, even if you are no a loyal Alabama fan, you know that the answer to that question would become a very emphatic "Yes", that not only would that young man grow up to follow in his father's footsteps at the University of Alabama, but then go on to a Hall of Fame career with the New England Patriots and general acclaim as the greatest offensive lineman of his era and one of the top few of all time. When I was a player in the late 70s and early 80s, and even into my coaching career some five years later, he was the gold standard for offensive line play, and to compare a player to John Hannah was to name him the best of his peers.

However, legends are for fans, and sometimes they hide the players who are at their core. As is my custom, I started the question portion of our interview by asking him about how he saw himself as a player in high school and how it affected his decision to go to Alabama out of Albertville High School. The answer was both fascinating and informative, and I think gives us a view of the man behind the legend.

It started with what I found to be a surprising and provocative admission. "I wasn't overly confident in my abilities. I wanted to play Pro Football like my dad, and there were several schools that were interested, but I wasn't sure if I was good enough." This in spite of a storied high school career at Baylor School in Chattanooga, Tennessee where he starred in football, track, and wrestling before transferring to Albertville for his senior campaign. "Football was my ticket out." That is both a challenge, and a heavy burden, and would become a centerpiece in all that he was to accomplish on the various football fields of his career, both the realization of his ability and the drive to always be the best.

But, like much that he shared with me, the story has much deeper roots, and those roots often led back to family and legacy, especially in terms of his father. Herb Hannah is a very important element of the John Hannah story, and in some ways, the father laid the groundwork for what the son would eventually construct.

"My Dad and Uncle played at Alabama, and my Dad would go on to be drafted by the New York Giants in 1951.

He grew up rough, the son of a sharecropper, and joined the Navy in 1942. He played on the service team, and he had a buddy named Rock McCants, who was from South Carolina, who kept trying to talk him into going to college after they got out. Dad kept telling him he wasn't smart enough, that he didn't have enough schooling to go to college, but finally, Rock got him to say yes. Then the question was where was he going to go? Rock told him he should go to Clemson with him.

Dad went to Clemson to talk to the coaches. They were interested, so he made them an offer. He had half his costs covered with his VA allotment, so he asked Clemson to cover the other half, give him a place to live and three meals a day. They said they could only do two.

That didn't work, but he remembered one of his coaches from the service team, Hank Crisp, had told him if he made it out alive and wanted to play some more ball, to look him up. Of course, Coach Crisp was at Alabama, so he called him, and went down to Tuscaloosa. He asked the same question, and they agreed. He was loyal to Alabama after that."

This set the stage for John's own decision at the end of his senior season. While many schools would have been eager

106

to have him, he cut his own list to three. Obviously, the University of Alabama, where his father and uncle had gone, the University of Georgia, where his father had been based for training and where he had met John's mother, a professor at the University, and in a bit of irony, Southern Cal, where his uncle had made some connections. It was a tough decision, but his father made it much clearer, if not easier.

"Dad pulled me aside one day and said, 'Wherever you go, I'll support you.' I told him thanks, Dad, and then he added, 'You do have to decide where you're going to eat when you come home, though'". The message was sent, and John was headed to Tuscaloosa, as were his brothers, Charley and David.

Once he donned the Crimson and White, it became apparent that his talents and demeanor would make him something special. Even in the pro-set offense of 1970, which was not ideally suited to his skillset at the time, and playing mostly offensive tackle, which required a lot of drop-back passing blocking techniques that were more passive and reactionary, it was obvious to all that his combination of size, quick feet, and that little bit of nasty set him apart.

"I was an offensive lineman with a defensive linemen's mindset. It was said about me, and I have to agree with it".

The sudden change to the wishbone offense in the fall of 1971 was almost an answer to prayer for Hannah. "Coming into fall camp, we had that meeting, and Coach Bryant told us we were putting in a new offense, the wishbone, and we couldn't tell anyone, had to keep it a secret until the first game. I was excited. It fit me. It was an OL's dream, just line up and go after folks. It was perfect for me, I was made to attack the other guy, to put my facemask in his face and drive him. The wishbone was easy, with a few plays with variations, but the techniques stayed mostly the same. No drop back pass blocking, didn't back up, just right at 'em."

There were three major programs that adopted the wishbone as their primary offense for much of the 1970s, though others would utilize it for portions of the era. The originators, the Texas Longhorns under coach Darryl Royal, were a power-based attack, while the Oklahoma Sooners, under coach Chuck Fairbanks, who we will encounter again later, opted for a more speed-based approach, living on the corners of defenses. Alabama under Bryant and Moore would be somewhere in between, though definitely more to the Texas end of the spectrum early on. Later, in the late 70s Alabama would add motion, spread alignments, and a much more integrated passing attack, but during Hannah's time, it was a ground and pound attack that could wear an opponent down and sap his will.

As we have discussed in other chapters, the offense was a fit for most of the team. Hannah agreed with my premise that the switch to the wishbone benefited the defense as it retooled and refit after the disappointments of the late 60s, and that it returned the team to the game control mode that Bryant preferred. It also featured the talents and skills of the multiple running backs on the roster and the particular abilities of their leader and quarterback.

"We had the perfect quarterback. Terry Davis was not only a great leader and player, but he had great vision. Good eyes, both in what he saw and in his peripheral vision. Sometimes you would watch the film and wonder how he saw things, how he picked up players outside of the normal field of vision. He was also a really good athlete.

Of course, we had all those good running backs. All of them could run the ball, and they were unselfish and would block hard for each other. It helped to wear the other team down and gave us balance. Beck, LaBue, Bisceglia, and of course, Musso. It played to our strength."

Like all such things, there were costs to go along with those benefits. "I will tell you a game I remember. We played

Southern Miss in Birmingham. We would get the ball on our 20, get four or five yards a play, work the ball down the field 12, 13, or 14 plays, then make a silly mistake, a penalty, a fumble, stop ourselves, and turn it over or miss a field goal. They would run three plays, get nothing, and then Ray Guy, one of the best punters of all time, would boom a sixty-yarder and we would have to start again on the 20 and do it all over. They talk about wearing the defense down on those long drives, but the offensive line gets worn down too. We went in at half-time and Coach Bryant chewed us out, said we were embarrassing ourselves. It was tough on them, but it could be tough on us too."

During that 1971 season and the run-up to the Auburn game, two games stuck out to Hannah. The first was obviously the game in Los Angeles, against the Trojans, who had throttled the Tide the year before in Legion Field. "They beat the snot out of us the year before, and it gave us great confidence for the whole season, to go out there and grab a lead and hang on against a really good team like that." A recurring theme in our conversation about that team and the teams to follow was the idea of confidence, of what you can rely on, and what counted in the pinch.

"I think being able to run the wishbone really fit us as a unit. It was who we were. The fit of that offense gave us confidence in the scheme. Confidence in the scheme equals confidence in yourself, and each other. It instilled in us a belief that the opponent couldn't beat us. They did sometimes, but we always believed we were going to win the game."

The other game that stood out to him was the LSU game in Baton Rogue. "It was one heck of a ballgame. They were very good, had a lot of good players, and a very tough place to play. Early on we punted. I played on the coverage team, and you know how sometimes the crowd noise can tell you what is happening even if you can't see it yourself. I heard the crowd roar change, and I thought the ball had gone through the endzone, so I let up and went into a trot. Tommy Cassanova, who was a great safety and an All-Pro in the NFL, he caught me and hit me, and knocked me on my butt. That got a really big crowd roar."

As for the Auburn game, his memories are crisp and concise. "It was a big game. We were ready to play that game. We were confident that we would win. We knew Sullivan and Beasly were very good, but we felt like they weren't a complete team, and we wanted to keep pressure on Sullivan for the whole game. With Mitchell and Parkhouse on the outside, little Terry Rowell, and the rest of that defense playing well, it bottled them up.

We were the more complete team. Terry and the backs and the ends, we could run and pass. And, of course, there was Musso doing what he did even on a bad toe. Like Coach Bryant said, 'Johnny could run for more yards on one leg than most could on two.'"

Several of the men I had the honor of speaking with have stories about that moment when they received the seal of approval from Coach Bryant, that phrase "you're a winner", but Hannah told me that he never felt that he and Bryant had that moment. Not all men who battle together, no matter their successes as a whole, find that personal bond, but I do know from talking to others for background on this book that Coach Bryant later expressed some concern that he had not made that connection with the man he often referred to as "the greatest lineman he had ever coached."

When I asked him if he had anything he wished people knew about him or his career, he was at first very hesitant. I had been told by several others I had talked to about the book when I mentioned that I was trying to schedule an interview with Hannah, that he is a private man and not given to talking about those times freely. I didn't have great expectations for an answer to a more personal inquiry, but after an initial negative response, when I explained how asking Gary Rutledge that question had changed the trajectory of the first book, he chuckled and then gave me several interesting memories that I would like to share.

"That reminds me of the two proudest moments of my career. The first was the time my Dad finally told me he was proud of me. I'm in my mid-twenties, several years into my pro career, and we would watch my games and he would talk to me about what I had done well and what I needed to do better. We played the Cowboys, and I had to block Randy White, who was a monster, and I have a really good game against him. After we watched the film, he usually had things to say, but he was quiet, and then he said 'You had a ___ of a game, a real ___ of a game'. Nothing else, but he was proud of me, and that was a real highlight for me. He didn't have any corrections or criticisms.

The second was a conversation I had with my line coach with the Patriots, Jim Ringo. I don't know if you remember, but he was the center for the Packers under Lombardi. He wasn't very big, but he was tough and he was smart and I loved playing for him. One day, after we had set the NFL rushing record in New England, I was talking with

Ringo and I asked him, 'Coach, do you think I could have played when you played?' And he answered me, 'John, there is no question about it.' You have to understand, those guys were my idols and they were tough and gritty and played a style of football I respected, and for him to say that was a very proud moment for me. I mean, if you could play then, you could play anytime. That was a thrill."

John Hannah played for a lot of coaches, many of them highly thought-of. At Baylor School, he played for Major Luke Worsham, whom he credited in his Hall-of-Fame speech. Then there would be Bryant, Ringo, his first offensive line coach in New England Red Miller, and in a very real sense, his father his whole life. But, he volunteered the fact that, in his opinion, the greatest coach he ever played for was his head coach when he arrived in New England, the aforementioned Chuck Fairbanks.

"He was the best. He had a great eye for talent, both players and coaches. He wasn't afraid of hiring coaches who might outshine him, he wanted the best. He respected you and wanted you to respect him. He left the Patriots because ownership would not let him keep his word to his players, wouldn't let him be a man of integrity, which he always was.

My rookie year, he called me into his office. He met with every player. He asked me, 'John, what do you want to do with your career?' I told him I wanted to win a Super Bowl, to be a champion. He said, 'John, everyone wants that, what do YOU want to do with YOUR career?' I told him, Coach, I have always dreamed of being the best O-lineman in football. 'How do you do that?' I thought about it and said 'Coach, I have to work very hard and commit myself to it, but I also need the kind of coach to teach me and correct me and get the very best out of me. He said, 'Then John, you work hard and tell me if you have a position coach that doesn't meet that standard.

Now that first year, my coach was Red Miller, who was a very successful line coach and had made a name with some of the good Cardinals offensive lines, so everything was great. Then, after that season, he got the Denver job, and we brought in a new guy. He was not a good coach, didn't do his job, and had some off-field issues we found out about later, so I went by Coach Fairbanks's office after the season and said, 'Coach, you remember that talk we had when I was a rookie?' He said, 'Yes, John I do.' I said, 'Coach, this guy isn't it.' All he said was 'Thanks'"

When we came back the next season, that guy was gone, and Jim Ringo was our coach. He taught me things I had never known and got the very best out of me. He got more out of me than even I thought I had."

All-American, All-Pro, Hall-of-Famer. The best of his time and his position. Crimson legend and fan-favorite. Husband, father, coach, businessman, farmer. All of these things, and something more. A young man, blessed with size and strength and agility, burdened by legacy and expectations and driven by a dream and drive to be the very best that he could be, and the best there was. Not made to back up, but to attack, to dominate the man and the situation before him, and to find, I hope, satisfaction in a dream achieved, a standard met, and the challenge conquered.

Second Quarter

The second block of the season on the Plains was a little less challenging for the Tigers, as they faced Southern Miss, Georgia Tech, and Clemson, with only the Yellow Jackets away from home. After the four-quarter battle in Knoxville, these games were all more slanted towards the Tigers in terms of talent and ability, as well as depth, and Auburn was able to roll through the three without any undue stress, reaching 5-0 and remaining undefeated in the Conference.

The one slight blip on the screen was a rather lackluster effort against the gritty Southern Miss squad in a 27-14 victory. There was probably no real moment when the upstarts from Hattiesburg were in an actual position to steal the game from the highly ranked Tigers, but the overall effort and the general effect of the game caused the AP to drop them one spot back down to five. A matter-0f-fact 31-14 thumping of the Yellow Jackets in Atlanta, a team that preseason was considered a potential challenge, stabilized the national perception of the program, and a routine 35-13 thrashing of an overmatched Clemson squad made the Southern Miss result look like an outlier.

The real story of this three-game run was the play of Sullivan and Beasley, and the national perception of Sullivan as a leading Heisman candidate. His numbers were noteworthy, if not always elite, but his obviously special athleticism and his flair for the splash play, enhanced by Jordan's big-play mentality and the efforts of Beasley and Schmalz, made an impression on fans and sportswriters. The weekly highlight shows, both regional and national, feature several clips of Sullivan escaping rushers, running for big yards, and slicing up defensive secondaries with derring-do. Heading into the second half of the season, he was numbered among the four or five favorites to bring home the coveted trophy.

Alabama entered the second quarter of its season with high momentum, and the surge continued to rise. First came a 40-6 annihilation of Ole Miss, a team that had been a thorn in the side of the Tide over the last three years. The game was never in doubt, and the Rebels seemingly had little or no answer for the wishbone and its multiple option concepts. The next game saw a 42-0 whitewashing of Vanderbilt in Nashville, a harbinger of things to come in this series for many years, as the Commodores were totally outclassed and never competitive.

This left the annual contest with the Tennessee Volunteers, the true number one rival for Bryant and his program. The Tennessee program under legendary coach Robert Neyland was famous for its physicality and suffocating defense, and provided a model for some of Bryant's vision of what a championship program should be. In the '60s and '70s, under the leadership of Doug Dickey, Bill Battle, and Johnny Majors, Tennessee was the standard for Alabama achievement, the traditional "third Saturday in October" meeting the measure of a player and a team to both programs.

In 1971, a very good Volunteers team under the guidance of Bryant pupil Bill Battle, which would finish the season with a 10-2 record marred only with losses to Auburn and Alabama, and with season-ending wins over fifth-ranked Penn St. and eighteenth ranked Arkansas in a Liberty Bowl tussel, came to Birmingham with a rock-solid defense and a tough, physical, if not prolific, offense. Early in the game, the teams traded turnovers and mistakes, and the Volunteers took advantage of a missed extra point to take a brief lead, but eventually Alabama took control behind several patented Musso runs, twisting and dragging defenders for extra yards, some accurate passing from Davis, and a defense which, boa-like, slowly squeezed the life out of the boys from Knoxville. The final was 32-15, and marked Alabama as not just a resurgent program, but one with the necessary components to challenge at the highest levels.

On the field in Birmingham, the second quarter would be primarily remembered as the time of correction. With a combination of ball control, opportunism, and inspired defense, especially the open-field efforts of cornerback Steve Willams, Alabama had held the Heisman trophy winner in check, but the first snap of the second quarter reminded everyone why he won it and why some thought his favorite receiver should have been in the conversation. The magic was back, at least for one play, as on third-and-nine, Sullivan faded deep, at last got some solid protection, and lofted a beautiful, arching pass which dropped expertly into the waiting arms of a streaking Beasley down the right sideline, a catch made difficult by the way the ball dropped out of the sky right over his head. It was good for 40 yards and was so reminiscent of the third-and-long and late-game heroics that had ripped the hearts out of opponents over the last three years, and especially those in Crimson, that a collective shudder had to have passed over the red half of Legion Field.

The Tigers were in business, down only two scores with an explosive, high-scoring offense and the ball at the opposition's 29. Here was a chance for Auburn to jump right back in the game, and to jump-start their high-octane passing game.

It was not to be. Two inside runs produced very little, and a third-down pass to Robinette was incomplete because Sullivan was under heavy pressure, a trend that would prove consistent for almost the entire game. Jordan, sensing that his team needed to snatch some momentum and the need to stay in contact with the Tide on the scoreboard, rolled the dice as he was wont to do and went for it on fourth down. Whether whatever play the Tigers chose had a chance will never be really known, as Sullivan, expecting more heavy pressure, pulled out from under center without the ball and Terry Rowell recovered the ball at the Alabama 28-yard line.

However, having escaped the first Auburn thrust towards the goal line, the Tide immediately returned the favor. On first down, fullback Ellis Beck slashed over right guard and on being hit from both sides, lost control of the football and the Tigers gleefully pounced on it.

This time, the Plainsmen did not waste the opportunity, digging into their trick bag and coming up with a 31-yard halfback pass from Harry Unger to Beasley, who was streaking wide open behind a bamboozled secondary. Gardner Jett knocked the extra point through and the game was now 14-7 in favor of the Tide.

The rest of the quarter really hinged on two Alabama possessions, as the Tigers were unable to generate any serious offensive threats. The first started right after the Auburn score, beginning with a nice kickoff return by Bobby McKinney to the Alabama 32. Davis returned to the counter option, which took advantage of the Auburn strength of pursuit and lateral quickness, for six yards, but two subsequent Musso carries left Alabama one yard shy.

Bryant, displaying his gambler side, went for it from his own 42, and a Davis sneak gained two and moved the sticks. Musso, continuing to rise above his painful injury, carried the ball to the Auburn 43, and the Tide seemed to be rolling towards another score, but a five-yard penalty pushed them off schedule, and despite a nice ten-yard completion to Wheeler on the pass off the counter option look, the drive ended fruitlessly after a Davis fumble and another Auburn recovery.

After a couple of punts, Alabama had one other opportunity. Taking over on their own twenty, they got things started with a couple of carries netting nine yards, but Auburn seemingly ended the drive with a strong stop of LaBue on third-and-one. However, the Tigers absorb a five-yard penalty for illegal substitution, and Davis, as he so often did, took full advantage with another nine-yard gain on a swing pass to LaBue in the flats. Bisceglia rode the advantage of the growing Bama dominance upfront for a sixteen-yard carry on the fullback give, and even a Davis slip on an attempted bootleg, losing six, was erased with a Musso halfback pass to Wheeler for seventeen and the first down.

The drive continued, with Davis hitting Bailey on a sprint out for twelve more yards and a first down. Davis, without the acclaim and certainly the numbers of Sullivan, was outplaying him within their respective systems. Of course, the talent in his backfield and at receiver, the dominance of the offensive line, and the ability of the Alabama defense to limit Sullivan's options and contain Beasley were huge contributing factors, but Davis, as he often did during his two years under center in Tuscaloosa, rose magnificently to the occasion and out-performed his more renowned adversary, and that was certainly true on this day.

With time running out, Musso sprang LaBue with a crushing block for seven, and, after a quick sideline throw to stop the clock, one of only two incompletions on the day, and a sprint to the right, the drive failed to live up to its expectations as Bill Davis, a good kicker, missed a 31-yard field goal attempt. At the half, the Tide, though dominant in most aspects, still led by only 14-7. The hopes of those who cried "War Eagle" were still alive, if somewhat bruised and battered.

The Defenders

Defense. It had long been the bedrock of the Bryant method, the ability to dominate an opponent and keep them out of the endzone, to create turnovers and win field position. His championship-level teams in the 1960's at the Capstone, as well as those he crafted in Lexington and College Station, were built on defense, fundamentals, conditioning, and toughness.

There is a summary of the Alabama defensive philosophy that has appeared in several places, but as far as I can determine, originated as an introduction in one of Bryant's defensive playbooks. It declares that defense is the part of the game that gives a player the best opportunity to express physical dominance of their opponent, a point of commonality between Bryant and current Alabama head coach Nick Saban. It outlined the four essentials of controlling the blocker so that the defender could disengage and pursue the ball, to do so rapidly and effectively, and for the secondary to defend the pass, particularly the deep pass, the long gain that could turn a game. This was paired with what amounted to the "commandments"; if they can't score they can't win, mistakes tend to follow the ball, weather is more of an issue for the offense than the defense, and the one that often surprises the reader, defense has more ways to score than the offense. If you doubt; blocked kick, intercepted pass, safety, recovered fumble, and punt return, which was primarily considered a defensive function at the time.

This was followed by a full page or more of axioms, some of which include: (1) the best players get blocked infrequently, but real players, no matter their level, don't stay blocked. (2) the value of a defensive player is inversely proportional to his distance from the ball. (3) it is imperative that each defensive player be aware of the down, distance, and game situation on every play. (4) a ball in the air belongs to the man who can obtain it, and a single interception could nullify several completions if the defense was effective in preventing long scoring plays. (5) the best and most effective defense resulted from eleven players playing with determination and physicality and a single purpose.

Then came the 1968, 1969, and 1970 teams. While their numbers are in no way poor or catastrophic, compared to the level of their predecessors and in relation to the Bryant model of football, the results were fatal to championship dreams. With the evolution of the game, and the rules changes which were being implemented during the era, offenses were almost guaranteed to produce more yards and explosive plays, but the key to Bryant's scheme was the ability to keep opponents out of the end zone. And this is where the changes become most apparent.

Alabama allowed an average of 4 points a game in 1966, a team many consider to be possibly Bryant's best during the decade, and some increase had to be expected but the numbers increased notably from '67-70. (11.9-12.6-24.4-22.0). They are indicative of an inability to establish game control, which limited the effectiveness of execution, depth, and conditioning, keys to the Bryant process.

The numbers, as is so often the case, both illuminate a situation and concurrently obscure some of its foundational issues. There were elements of recruiting and scheme that contributed to the alarming rise in scoring, as the increase in the athletic pool with the inclusion of African-American athletes in major college programs, and the rules and ideas evolutions mentioned above required adjustments in techniques, packaging of players and most definitely in recruiting. These adjustments were in progress in Tuscaloosa, but a key element to the change in scoring defense can be traced to the offensive scheme. By focusing more on an attempt to establish a controlled passing game and feature more "explosive" plays, Alabama's scoring numbers improved as well, and passing and total yardage soared to unseen levels, but there was a reduction in their ability to control the cloak, field position, and possession of the ball. It put an emphasis on athletes and individual plays and forced Alabama to take more chances and thus make more mistakes, creating opportunities for the opponent.

In 1971, the trend began to move back in the other direction. The staff and recruiting changes began to bear fruit, and Alabama began to accumulate the depth and talent to reestablish its defensive dominance. By the end of the decade, Tide defenses would again be at the top of the national food chain, and the turn was obvious even at the earliest dates.

A major contributor was the style of play available in the wishbone and a triple-option concept. In *Crimson Fraternity,* Terry Davis related an attempt to use tempo and hurry-up principles against Florida to take advantage of the way they adjusted to the width of the field and their manner of calling defenses, which gassed the offense and was not repeated. The wishbone could and did use tempo changes, but it gave the offense, similar to today's spread attacks, the ability to dictate tempo to defenses, especially if it could produce four yards plus on first down. The constant threat of the fullback running pretty much straight ahead for chunks of yards had to be accounted for, even if you feared the outside elements more. This resulted in defenses that became spread thinner laterally than they were accustomed to, and created seams for the quarterback and the halfbacks to cut quickly and gash the defense. Add in the fact that option football created a lot of one-on-one opportunities for the wideouts and tight end, which produced high averages on reception if fewer numbers of them, and the offense could produce scoring numbers similar to the best of the more air-oriented version.

All of this helped the developing defense by limiting their exposure, often allowing them to play from ahead which further limited offensive options, and forced the game into the style they were designed to play. It is my personal opinion that this potential result had a large impact on Bryant's thought process in making the change.

Of course, no scheme will succeed without talent and execution, and Alabama was beginning to harvest the results of the personnel and concept changes. Jeff Beard, John Mitchell, Robin Parkhouse, and Terry Rowell manned the down linemen positions, and with their mix of physicality, quickness, and aggression, they were highly effective. Mitchell was a rare mix of quickness and strength, Rowell was toughness personified, Beard was steady and consistent, and Parkhouse was headed for pro greatness when a combination of a devastating knee injury and personal issues sidelined that arc. But, for that season, and especially for that game, he was magnificent.

Linebackers Jeff Rouzie, Chuck Strickland, and Tom Surlas were talented and tough, but it was their ability to play as a unit, with seemingly one mind, that created difficulty for opponents and proved an unsolvable puzzle for Sullivan, Beasley, and their mates. They reacted in unison and covered when any member took a risk and were a master course in playing together at the second level.

The addition of Bill "Brother" Oliver as secondary coach, lured from the Auburn plains, in combination with Pat Dye, Richard Williamson, and coordinator Ken Donahue, had 'Bama prepared all season, and that level of readiness came to a peak against the Tigers. The "Steves", Higginbotham, Wade, and Williams, along with Lanny Norris, formed a cohesive and fundamentally sound unit, and their ability to play man-help and combination zone coverages took away a lot of the short and medium timing routes from the Auburn offense, not only limiting their production but forcing improvisation that led to two key second-half interceptions by

Strickland and Rouzie that helped to finish the game off. Watching the video, and comparing it to others of the period, you can see quite a few subtle innovations that often go unnoticed.

Auburn's defense was a solid unit themselves. Built primarily on quickness and gang tackling, using a layered approach with orderly pursuit angles and feeding off their productive and explosive offense, they could afford to play softer zone coverages combined with active, slanting fronts, which tended to leave their linebackers free to roam. Bob Brown and Tommy Yearout up front, Mike Flynn and Mike Neal at linebacker, and Dave Beck and David Langer in the secondary all made plays during the season, and the entire defense was built on surrendering yards but limiting big plays and preventing touchdowns, which was not dissimilar to the Alabama premise, though the style was different.

But, there was a difference going into the Iron Bowl. Auburn had been very successful against some of the good teams early in their schedule who were talented but one-dimensional. However, they did show signs of stress later in the year when teams had more film to study, and against Mississippi State and Georgia, teams more adapted to threaten them in varieties of ways, they gave up significantly more yards and points. The wishbone, at this time, threatened defenses in more complex ways than almost anything since the heyday of the Notre Dame box, with its shifts, motions, and multiple run/pass threats. Having to play assignment football and to account for Davis' ability to scramble and throw on the run caused stress and threatened to disrupt the pursuit angles and multi-level approach of the Tigers, would prove to be a bridge-too-far for them on this day.

"If it's easy, then you don't want it." It was a quote of
Coach Bryant's that Robin Parkhouse shared with me, one of
several that cropped up during our interview. It's one that you
don't hear near as often as many of his others, but after
reflecting on our conversation, I thought it an apt way to start
this chapter. Like so many of the players from that 1971 team,
Parkhouse is quick to quote or attribute life values and
standards to Coach Bryant, even some fifty years after that
impactful season. It is not only a mark of the man they knew
as "Coach" but a common foundation of the men they
became. These weren't just words, they were elements of a
core philosophy that stretched far beyond the playing fields
and the locker rooms.

When I asked Robin what drew him to Alabama as a
decorated high school player, his answer was direct and to the
point. "I wanted to play for the toughest coach, the best, the
one who wanted to win championships. The one who would
get the best out of me." During his career at the Capstone,
Bryant would prove to be that man, and Parkhouse would
become a dominant force from his defensive end position.

From the very beginning of our conversation, Parkhouse was a firm proponent of the basic argument I am making with this work. Like the author, he sees the 1971 season as integral to the dominant decade that would follow, not only in terms of setting a standard, or more to the point, re-establishing the one that had existed in Tuscaloosa for almost all of Coach Bryant's tenure but in reinvigorating the legend's vision for Alabama football and his place in it.

"We were fortunate to be there at that time. I once heard Johnny Musso talk about how the wishbone really re-invigorated Coach Bryant. It was in his wheelhouse, you had to hit people and be physical. You had to block for each other be unselfish, be dedicated, and never quit. You outworked and outhit the other guy, and used the talents that you had. It was what he believed in."

The success of the program and the "Bryant way" had a cost. The practices, and even the off-season program, were tough. Those who had been with Bryant over the years equated the worst of them with some of his earlier practices, even to some degree back to the time spent in Junction, Texas Not everyone could handle this level of intensity and physicality and conditioning, but those that did survive, those who were determined to do things the way Bryant envisioned them, were promised a path to victory and success, and they found it.

"Win the one-on-one battles and be physical. It fit him and it fit us. He was trying to find out if you wanted to win his way, and those who were left were part of something special."

In conducting these interviews and talking to these men, it struck me, again and again, the incredible bond that unites them even to this day, some fifty years hence. Not just a general fondness and the occasional reunion or gathering, but a daily connection and a shared sense of place and accomplishment. This quote from Robin may go a long way to explaining why this is so. The shared pride of overcoming something beyond the scope of normal commitment and teamwork, and the understanding that in doing so, they gained much more than accolades, trophies, or the treasured memories of fans over the generations. They acquired a commitment to excellence and brotherhood that shapes and enriches them to this day. In conducting my interviews and occasional follow-ups with these men, I have been exposed to the merest shadow of this, and even that small glimpse has proven life-altering to me. I can only imagine and admire the full effect it has had on these men over the intervening years.

Within the first ten minutes of our conversation, after we had shared a mutual begrudging respect for modern technology and a stubborn clinging to as much of our original ways and means as possible, Parkhouse, in his own style, stated my main premise and belief without the least prompting on my part.

"If we hadn't had the turnaround in '71, he (Bryant) might have retired or gone on to the NFL. He couldn't stand being average, and he bore down on that group. The lesson was simple; 'Never Quit.'"

As difficult as the 1970 season had been, Parkhouse did identify one element that would help lead to the defensive turnaround in 1971. There were a significant number of sophomores who contributed in that season, and their growing maturity as players, coupled with their growth physically under the demanding off-season routine, created a group poised to re-establish the Tide as a dominant and fearsome defense, the hallmark of Bryant-led teams.

"We had a lot of young guys that played the year before, and the embarrassment of that season and the change and challenge of the preparation leading up to the '71 season sparked some of them and their attitudes towards the team and the game. The wishbone helped, it gave us time, and adding Coach Oliver helped pull it all together. Do you know what was a huge factor for that team, and especially for the defense? I am sure as a player and a coach you have seen it and felt it, but when it starts happening around you it's electric. We gained momentum, from the workouts and a sense of being something special, and then we went out to Los Angeles and beat that USC squad after they kicked our butts the year before, that momentum and that feeling just carried on through the year and got to be more and more a part of us."

Robin also agreed with me that it is a mistake to try and separate the offense from the defense in trying to evaluate what happened within the team and the program in that fateful 1971 season. There was, is often the case, a deep and important synergy within that group, on both sides of the ball, in terms of what was occurring. The wishbone allowed Alabama to control the pace of the game and to often dictate field position and reduced significantly the number of snaps played by the defense. The defense, as it became more mature and melded some of its new concepts within the standards of a

Bryant defense, eliminating long scoring plays and forcing the opposition to be more disciplined and fundamentally sound than they might like, gave the offense time to find its rhythm and overcome occasional errors. Additionally, the mix of personnel and leadership that evolved from the cauldron of two disappointing seasons and the fire of that summer of 1971 became something beyond just accumulated talent and experience.

"The timing was very fortunate. We had two great players, Musso and Hannah. We had a lot of very good players, but those two were just different. Coach Bryant knew how to recognize the abilities and attitudes of others, like Terry Davis. Coach Bryant saw his skillset and just built around that. Terry was amazing in reading the defense and he was so quick with his feet. He could throw it too, better than some people thought and good enough for us, and David Bailey was very good. David is a good example of that team. He had been a great receiver, caught a lot of passes with Scott Hunter there when we threw the ball a lot, or a lot for those days, and he loved catching the ball. Good speed and a student of route running, just a great route runner. It seemed like he always caught the ball. I don't remember him ever dropping one, in a practice or game, though I am sure he did.

When we shifted to the wishbone, David became more of a blocker. He still caught some balls, and made some big catches that year, but he just became a great blocker and never complained. Never made it about him, just did what the team needed and helped us win."

Not to quibble with Robin, but I have to insist that there were three "great" players on that team, and one of them wore the number ninety jersey in Crimson and White. He was as integral a part of that team as any, capable of dominating offensive lineman and wrecking the plans of the opposition. And, in the Auburn game, he would display all of those abilities.

Robin went on to discuss just how unusual that 1971 season was in college football, not just for Alabama and Auburn, but for the Oklahoma Sooners and the Nebraska Cornhuskers as well. The two Big 8 foes at the time also approached their traditional year-end meeting undefeated and untied, and the combination of four teams, in two conferences, in that identical state on the last weekend of the season foreshadowed the current playoff scenarios. Even with the bowl pairings already ordained before those games, it was a lock that the eventual national champion would emerge from the two regular-season matchups and the two bowl game contests. One of these four would wear the crown, and if the football public were lucky, it would come down to the two undefeated survivors in a head-to-head meeting. And, of course, it did.

Heading into the battle in Birmingham, with so much riding on the outcome, and with the fresh and painful memories of the previous two meetings and the heroics of Sullivan and Beasley, Parkhouse recalled the preparation of the coaching staff, the commitment to end the Tigers winning streak, and the drive to be the champions that Bryant had told them they could be.

"As good as Coach Bryant was, we also had a great staff overall. Just tremendous coaching. So many of them went on to great coaching careers of their own, and when Coach Bryant came in and gave us the 'sink or swim' speech, they bought right in and really worked with us on the field. In that Auburn game, we were the most prepared team I have ever been on. They had a well-planned approach for us, and we felt like we were ready for everything Auburn did. Brother did a great job, just gave us so many little things and helped us get ready. The coaches had so many things for us to key on and read, just the most prepared we ever were.

I'll give you an example, an important one. Coach Oliver noticed that Sullivan had a lower release than normal, just a little but he threw from around his shoulder height instead of up around his ear. When we saw that, when we saw him gather up and get ready to throw, we practiced raising up, getting our hands up, and trying to get in his sight, and we knocked down several. I got a couple and so did some of the others. It affected him, and we were ready for it."

It was a total team effort. Robin was a little hesitant to mention teammates, afraid that he would skip someone or an important play and give the impression of lessening the contribution of any, but he mentioned the overall play of the defensive line in controlling the Auburn running game and keeping Sullivan from finding a comfort zone, the outstanding play of the linebacker corps in chasing Sullivan when he scrambled, controlling the screen and check-down game to the running backs, and the two interceptions which helped to salt the game away, and of course the sparkling play of the secondary in limiting the contributions of Beasley and Schmalz, with a special nod to the efforts of the speedy and athletic Steve Williams who drew the coverage assignment on Beasley most often, and whose three key tackles a yard short of the sticks helped stymie any potential momentum for the Auburn offense. In the end, they controlled the explosive Tiger attack and let the methodical offense grind them into the Legion Field turf.

After gaining their revenge and slaying the Sullivan-Beasley dragon, it was off to that hoped-for #1 versus #2 meeting with the Cornhuskers, which did not go as they had hoped and planned but continued the process that would lead to three national titles in the '70s and the potential for others. "We won the SEC that year, got our championship rings for that, but we caught a real good Nebraska team and that one didn't turn out like we wanted. It set the standard, and showed we could win doing it Coach Bryant's way."

And, that brings me to the last two questions of the interview and the heart of what Robing Parkhouse shared with me. In response to my question regarding what it was about Bryant that drove his players and coaches to strive for perfection and to value his approval above their own comfort and dreams, he was at first hesitant.

"I always feel like I do a woeful job of answering that question. I get asked about that pretty often, and I don't know if I have a good answer."

Then, after a few minutes of reflection, he gave me an answer so comprehensive in scope and so revealing of how he still relates to the man who was more than just his coach that, despite the conventions of professional writing, I am going to quote it as fully as possible below. To do otherwise would be criminal.

"For me, it was his character, his presence. It was like no one else I had ever seen. He could fill up a room all by himself. We just believed him, that voice of his, his way of speaking to you. When we survived that summer, those of us that did, we believed him even more. He convinced us that he had the formula for winning, for being champions. And, he did.

I think it was maybe the last conversation I had with Mal Moore before he passed, and we were talking about Coach Bryant. I said, 'Coach Moore, if we learned anything from Coach Bryant, it was like that old saying, when the going gets tough, the tough get going.' He laughed and said, '___ right we did.'

And, just to never quit. To keep going. You just kept going. He had a way of motivating us to believe in each other and in what the coaches were teaching us. To believe in our way of doing it. He would say, 'You might be cussing me right now, but in the fourth quarter when the guy who has been whipping you all day starts to falter and you start to win, you'll thank me.' And, he was right.

Another thing. He really cared about us. I think he shares that with Coach Saban. He cared about us, not just as players or people who could help him win, but as young men, and later on. For all of our lives. I didn't always understand that back then or appreciate it all the time, but he wanted the best for us, in everything we did.

We all knew, to a degree anyway, that he was in reality a living legend. He had already won championships and won trophies. We all knew that, it was a big part of why most of us were there. Then, there were the two down years and it wore on him some, but we were part of turning it around and bringing it back where it was supposed to be. He carried all of that on his shoulders, the demands and expectations, every day. You knew that if you gave him everything you had, and the extra he knew was there, he would make you successful. It was what made him different, that way he had of making you sure that he knew how to make you and the team the best it could be."

And then, I asked the last question, the one I save for the end of my interviews, the one that gives me the most varied responses and some of the best things in either of the two books on the wishbone era I have now written. When I asked a man who is a Crimson Tide legend, a successful businessman, and someone who survived not only that summer in the Alabama heat but the vagaries of life and some personal setbacks that might have crushed a spirit not buoyed by the lessons of Coach Bryant and his staff what would he like people to know about him that they might not know, he gave me an answer that will resonate with me for the rest of my life.

"The only thing, uh, … I'll just say this. The most important thing in my life, for a long time now, for 37 years, is that I asked Jesus Christ into my life in 1985. It is the best and most important decision in my life. It was the defining moment of my life. It was an eternal decision and one that I will never change. It changed everything.

The second most important thing in my life is finding my wife Sarah, 16 years ago. I met her at a church service, I had never been married, and she sustains me in every way."

Life has not always been easy for Robin Parkhouse. But, that is probably true for all of us, because life is important, and in the extension of the Bryant quote that led this chapter, the things worth having are the ones you work the hardest for. It was a lesson that he never really forgot, and despite the peaks and valleys of the human experience, it has brought him to a place of strong and lasting fellowship with his teammates, an affirming marriage to his soulmate, and a faith that, in the words of several of his teammates who urged me to do all in my power to include him in this book, brought about as complete and astounding a conversion and regeneration as any had ever witnessed. The man I spoke with was humble, giving, and gracious, making my childhood admiration for his playing ability and fierce spirit of competition give way to my admiration for the man he has become. To my mind, Robin Parkhouse has become the very epitome of that quote, a man who truly appreciates what he has because he knows the price he paid for it. To borrow another old phrase I have grown fond of over the years, I wish him the joy of it.

Third Quarter

The final sprint of the regular season before the Iron Bowl found Auburn challenged twice, after a 40-7 thrashing of the Florida Gators at home. It was, in some ways, it was the most complete domination of a game for the Tigers all season, and the outcome was never seriously in doubt. It moved the conference record to 3-0 and set Jordan and his charges up for the final push against Mississippi State, Georgia, and, of course, Alabama.

The Bulldogs from Starkville were not considered a serious threat to the Tigers, but the combination of inspired play by the underdogs and sloppy, unfocused play for most of the game by Auburn led to a unconvincing 30-21 win. Sullivan, Beasley, and the running backs made enough plays to carry them to victory, but the style of play was enough to drop Auburn another spot to number six.

Of course, this set them up for the showdown they had been anticipating since they emerged victorious back in week two in Knoxville. Number six Auburn versus number seven Georgia in Athens, Georgia, two undefeated teams driven by very different but very impactful quarterbacks. Georgia hung their hat on quarterback Andy Johnson, a solid thrower but almost another tailback when carrying the ball, and a smothering Bulldog defense that had manhandled most of their opponents during the season.

However, there were some pundits who felt that the Bulldogs, as talented and accomplished as they were, might be a tad overrated because of the softness of their schedule. They had not faced many high-level offenses, and there were few teams on the schedule that were any better than slightly above average. Auburn would most definitely be a step-up in competition, while the Tigers had faced at least two quality teams.

The game is as renowned for its pregame shenanigans as it was for what transpired on the field. Over-eager Georgia students and fans decided it would enhance their cause to deny the Tigers rest before the game, so the night before the clash, there was a running cascade of pulled fire alarms, loud music blared from speakers positioned near the team hotel, and even cars circling the block with horns in full throat. Additionally, the day before, when the visiting team usually conducts a walk-through light practice, the weather was cold and windy, with snow flurries, limiting their preparation time.

The walk to the field left several Tigers soaked with a beer bath, but this only seemed to tighten their focus. Auburn jumped out to a 14-0 lead, as Sullivan ran and passed the Bulldogs dizzy. Spreading the defense wide and then hitting them deep, he exposed the cracks that no one else had the talent to do, and the Bulldogs seemed on the verge of being run off their own field, but Andy Johnson was not quite ready to bow out. Taking his team on his broad shoulders, he ran, passed, and improvised two scoring drives, and the game stood at 14-14.

Early in the fourth quarter, Auburn had forged ahead once again, 21-14, but yet again Johnson took the reins and willed his team to a score, capping it with a powerful two-yard run. The excitement of the Bulldog faithful was short-lived because Auburn's Roger Mitchell surged through the protection and blocked the extra point, preserving a one-point lead.

Sullivan, with gunslinger ferocity, made them pay immediately. On the first play after the kickoff, he whipped a dart to Beasley who split two defenders, as he had often done before, and sprinted seventy yards for the score. This was Sullivan's third scoring pass of the day, and his second to Beasley, and after a Tiger stop and a long punt return by Owens, Sullivan finished the game with his fourth touchdown pass to Schmalz. The game, and the Heisman, belonged to Pat

Sullivan, and his numbers on the day were indicative of his season and his gift. He completed 14-24, not noteworthy in itself, but accounted for 248 yards and four touchdowns, along with several key runs and some spectacular scrambles. The Tigers were 9-0 and 5-0 in conference, and with the Penn St. loss to Tennessee, ascended to number five in the nation. Alabama and its new wishbone offense and resurgent defense were all that stood in the way of a conference championship, an undefeated season, a date with Oklahoma in New Orleans that might be for a national title, and, even more importantly, a chance to lay claim to a state championship and the perception that they were now the top program in the South.

The last lap for Alabama also had its own challenges. A surprisingly competitive battle with a game Houston squad finished 34-20, with the Cougars presenting maybe the most difficult offensive challenge of the season, and then came what was, after the opener at USC, its stiffest challenge. LSU, under the leadership of Bryant protege Charlie McClendon, provided some approaches to defending the triple option and some of its offshoots that Alabama had not seen and did not have a lot of answers for. The game was a physical slugfest, but the improving defense showed its measure, Davis made several big plays in front of his home state fans, and the Tide survived the injury to Musso to win 14-7.

The penultimate regular season game of the 1971 season for the Crimson Tide was a 31-3 dismantling of an overmatched Miami Hurricane team, leaving the Crimson Tide at 10-0 and a matching 5-0 in conference, with all the conference and national possibilities in play as well. But, as they approached Legion Field and their date with the Tigers, they were also in quest of re-asserting their regional and national pedigree, and of reminding a watching national audience that Paul W. Bryant was still among the elite coaches of his or any other generation.

With the second-half kickoff, Auburn continued to try and find momentum. Trapping Williams at his sixteen on the return, the Tigers were hopeful of a quick three and a punt that would leave them with optimal field position, a hope that would not come to fruition. Musso, Bisceglia, and LaBue, behind their increasingly dominant front line, ripped off solid chunks of real estate, and Davis combined with LaBue again on a pass in the flats for a significant gain, eventually leading to a third-and-two, which became a third-and-seven after an untimely penalty. Davis, with only his second miss of the day, was unable to hook up with Bailey but Gant hit a textbook punt and LaBue downed it on the Auburn one.

In any contested game, there are a handful of moments when the game can turn. In many ways, the next Auburn possession, though it resulted in no points for either team, no big plays or turnovers, was a critical element of the outcome. Starting from their one, Sullivan and Beasley, with an assist from Robinette, worked the ball up to near midfield, with a succession of short, quick passes which seemed to bring the mostly dormant Tiger offense to life. Countering this was Alabama's exemplary open-field tackling, especially against Beasley, who had made a career of turning seven yards into seventy, along with a continued effective push of the defensive line, with two passes batted down to prevent completions, one by Parkhouse who was beginning to dominate his personal matchup and adversely affect the Auburn offense. Eventually, it ended when Sullivan hit Beasley on a screen pass in the right flats. With blockers in front and, finally, a chance to get up a full head of steam, the play looked like trouble for the Tide defense, but Strickland, following the lead of Williams and Rouzie, fought off a blocker and made a solid tackle one-on-one against the elusive and explosive wideout. Once again, a potential

Auburn drive had come a cropper one yard short, and the resultant Beverly punt was fair-caught by McKinney on the twenty-two.

While the result of the drive seems inconsequential, it would prove to be the only time Sullivan and Beasley would find any consistent rhythm, especially with the short passing game, and would effectively be the last gasp for a frustrated and flustered Tiger offense. They had finally found a means of at least getting the ball in the hands of their playmaker, but it was not productive, and Alabama did not wilt under the flurry.

The next drive, beginning from their twenty-two after the stop, was the beginning of the end. Utilizing the counter option concept again, Musso ripped off one of his signature runs, weaving and cutting on his injured foot for eighteen yards, seeming to be playing at a different speed than everyone else. The drive seemed to be coming to a premature end when two thrusts produced only a third-and-eight, but Davis proved that he could also produce some third-down magic himself, finding running room for a sixteen-yard gain. Bama went behind their dominant right side three times, but, just short of a first down, they tried it once again, Musso behind Hannah and mates, and the result was five hard-won yards and a first down. Davis closed the quarter with no gain, and the final fifteen was ahead, with the score still 14-7, but the weary and battered Tiger defense on the ropes.

Steve Sprayberry

Steve Sprayberry made his mark in the professional world as a successful insurance agent, to the point where he served as president of the Alabama Independent Insurance Agencies Association. This seems rather fitting for a man who made his mark in Alabama football lore as one of the men who insured the health and prosperity of the likes of Terry Davis, Gary Rutledge, Steve Bisceglia, Wilbur Jackson, and Ellis Beck, along with others as a backup lineman in 1971 and the starter at LT for the 1972 and 1973 seasons. With Steve Sprayberry on the field, they were all in good hands.

His path to Tuscaloosa had a few speed bumps. As an integral part of the Sylacauga Aggies state championship team, and a Super All-State selection, Steve garnered some interest from southern Universities, but the one offer he desired most was not forthcoming. When I asked him where he wanted to go as a decorated senior, the answer, so typical of our conversation, was simple and direct. "Alabama, always Alabama." Coach Mal Moore was his area recruiter, and he was friendly, but as a "tweener", a player with not the ideal size for a big man and not the quickness to play positions designed for smaller players, the offer did not materialize.

Coach Moore was not sure Steve was what they were looking for.

Fortunately, Sprayberry had an ace in the hole. His high school coach, former "Fullback of the decade" at Alabama Tom Calvin, had never pushed the Tide on him, but when Steve informed the coach that Tuscaloosa was his desired destination, Calvin made use of his connection to the program and made a call. Quickly, a highlight film made the journey to Tuscaloosa, and soon the desired offer was made. Coach Bryant remarked that "we search for players that football is important to all over the country, and here is one in our backyard. Sign him". Later, Coach Moore would remark that while he recruited Sprayberry, Coach Bryant picked him.

Sprayberry was willing but admittedly undersized, so the first order of business was to gain weight and strength. This meant an arduous program and long hours of intense work, but he told me that he never had any questions about his decision. "Alabama was the best place for me. The toughest environment and the greatest challenge."

The environment would get even tougher in the Spring of '71. Bryant was on a mission to return Alabama to its accustomed position of prominence, and that started with finding the type of players he could coach the best. The spring was tough, tougher than even the norm, and the wishbone had yet to make its appearance, but even it paled before the cauldron of the summer when the legendary coach begin to forge his new weapon. Almost all the players had jobs in the summer, some in Tuscaloosa and some back at home, and Steve was one of the latter, but the workouts and the running were for everyone.

When the team assembled as one before fall camp, the new program was revealed at the famous "sink or swim" meeting. "I didn't know anything about the wishbone, but Coach showed us the basics on the board, and I saw an opportunity. I wasn't good at drop-back pass blocking, but I could run block, and that is what was required." In an interview, Sprayberry did in April of 2020 with Kirk McNair of BamaOnLine, he related a story that illustrates the difference between switching from the pro-style passing attack of 1970 to the wishbone. "I was a left tackle, but it wasn't the same as it is now. I was at a meeting with Terry Davis a few years ago, and Terry introduced me to his wife, saying 'He had my blindside'. I started laughing because that doesn't mean the same now as it did when we were in the wishbone."

During the August practices, it was pretty obvious who the starters were, and even the "swing" players, but Coach Jimmy Sharpe, the offensive line coach, was upfront with the younger players. They were working and competing to see who would be aboard the flight headed to Los Angeles in a few weeks. In other words, who would make the travel squad and be in line to play that season? Steve was determined to be one of those fortunate few, and he made that dream come true

The 1971 season held some opportunities to play for the sophomore, but the biggest element of that year for him was the opportunity to prove himself to Coach Bryant and the staff. For those who didn't start or rotate every week, there was an added period after practice was over, a scrimmage between offense and defense that could last for forty-five minutes to even an hour, an intense period where no one held back and no quarter was given. It was a proving ground, and an opportunity to show the coaches that you were a "winner", a player who could be counted on to play the Bryant way no matter what.

It was here that the young Sprayberry, still a little undersized, earned the trust of his teammates and his coaches, and established himself as a "winner". The results were two years as the starting left tackle in 1972 and 1973, a national title and legacy that lives on today at the Capstone with his selection as All-SEC as a senior.

One of the basic premises of this book is that the 1971 season was a pivotal one in the resurgence of the Alabama football program, and in establishing what was to follow. Steve agreed with this, pointing out that Terry Davis would set the standard for wishbone quarterbacks at Alabama, which would be followed up by redshirt Gary Rutledge, who would refine the art of reading and distributing the ball in the offense, while Johnny Musso is, in the minds of many, still the gold standard for running backs in Tuscaloosa, and John Hannah remains a measuring stick for offensive linemen not only at the university but in the NFL as well.

During the current run of exceptional success at Alabama under Coach Nick Saban, fans often hear references to the "Alabama standard" but like almost everything in football (and in life), it is not new. Coach Bryant and the '71 Alabama Crimson Tide set the bar for all the success of the 70s and early 80s with their work ethic, their physicality, and their pride in being the very best they could be.

As for the Auburn game itself, he also acknowledged that it was an important hallmark, not only for fans as an indication of what had happened within the program but for the players themselves, especially those who would return for the next two seasons and beyond. "It would establish who we were and how we were going to do what we wanted to do. We had a clear plan for how we were going to keep winning, and we understood what was expected of us."

There were on-field rewards as well. "It showed the power of the wishbone, not only in scoring points but in ball control and owning the clock. The defense was so much better, not because of changes in personnel, though there were a few, but because we kept the ball and they were fresher and more aggressive."

His personal memories of the open week before the game were primarily of more preparation, more chances for the younger players to continue to improve and learn, to show that they were worthy of being "the next man up". Sprayberry recalled it this way. "That week was part of my process. Coach Bryant believed he was a winner, and he wanted to find out who his winners were. That open week was a lot of preparation, a lot of working to show him we were winners. That Auburn game was important, but mostly because it was the next game. I will tell you, I wasn't sure Musso would be able to play with that injury, but fortunately, he was".

The payoffs for Steve and his classmates would be plentiful over the next two years. In 1972, he was part of the miracle comeback in Knoxville, when the Tide scored 14 points in the final couple of minutes to snatch victory from the jaws of defeat. The Tennessee game was always big for Coach Bryant, the rival who provided a measuring stick for the type of player and team that wore Crimson in any given year. How you played against Tennessee was a window into how you would play in any other big game.

"That game, that comeback, was a team effort, with the special teams coming up big and the defense getting a stop when we had to have it, but when I watch that game, what I see, especially among the linemen, is the effort. Guys reaching down deep inside themselves to find something extra, that special something that lets you beat a good team on a bad day on their field. It bonded that team and gave us confidence in who we were. When we get together for our reunions, it gets discussed."

The following year, in Birmingham, another loss was dealt to the Volunteers, this time heralded by a bolt from a clear sky when Rutledge hit a streaking Wayne Wheeler for an 80-yard touchdown pass in route to a 42-21 Alabama victory. The play was the brainchild of Coaches Moore and

161

Sharpe, who spotted the Tennessee defense cheating up the backside safety against an option look, and diagrammed a pass to take advantage of it. As Sprayberry recalled, the process for suggesting something new was to draw it up for Coach Bryant on a Monday, explain why it would work, and then let it marinate with him for a bit. That Thursday, he informed the team they would open with it, and the rest is glorious Crimson history.

After an excruciating loss to the Auburn Tigers in 1972, when two blocked punts in the final moments overturned an afternoon of Tide dominance, Sprayberry and his classmates decorated their national championship senior season with a 35-0 thumping of Auburn. "In '73, we were just a very good football team. It wasn't about revenge, but simply a culmination of the first three years of the wishbone and the way Coach Bryant wanted us to play."

It wasn't always easy, but sometimes that just made it better. As good as they were in 1973, they had to come from behind to beat Georgia and trailed Kentucky 14-0 at the half. From the McNair interview on BamaOnLine, Steve recalled how this just provided another opportunity for Bryant to teach his men his way.

"At halftime of the Kentucky game, I still remember what Coach Bryant said. He said, 'I'm glad we are in this situation. A lot of people have been talking about y'all being a special bunch. We're fixing to find out how special y'all really are.'"

As usual, I asked Steve if there was anything he wanted people to know that he thought they didn't. After a moment or two to think, he replied this way. "People don't really understand how hard it was to earn the moniker 'winner' from Coach Bryant. How difficult it was, him standing behind you, not saying much, but enough. Encouraging you sometimes, challenging you at others, to be the best you could be. To find out who could push himself, who could finish the job."

The honesty and intensity of his answer prompted one additional question, something I had wondered about for a long time. I asked him if he could put his finger on what it was exactly about this man, this coach, that made everyone around him want to work and sacrifice so much to gain his approval? After confessing that there was no complete and comprehensive answer, like a true Bama man he gave it his best.

"Certainly, you wanted to please him. When he came down out of that tower when you heard those chains swing together, everyone snapped to attention. He might be mad, might be coming down to chew on someone and you didn't want to be that person, but a lot of times he just wanted to be closer to the team, to be in the middle of what we were doing. Every play, everybody glanced out of the corner of their eye to see how he was responding to what you had done. If it was good, you got his approval and felt like a winner, but if it was bad you just wanted to find a place to hide."

I have mentioned in other places how much the close-knit relationships of this team have impressed me, and Steve and his wife are a large part of that. They host a reunion at their lake house, and he, like so many others from those early years of wishbone-era football, stays in close contact. He related a story to me from Wilbur Jackson, whose move from wide receiver to running back led to not only stardom at Alabama but a lengthy and successful NFL career. Jackson meets his pro teammates from time to time, but those brief encounters are not like being among his Alabama brothers. Fifteen minutes of catching up are not like hours of reminiscing.

Steve Sprayberry went from All-state to All-SEC. He went from state champion to national champion. He went from ensuring the safety of Davis, Rutledge, and Musso to ensuring the well-being of his friends and neighbors. But, through it all, he proved time and time that he truly was a "winner".

David Knapp

In writing the story of a college football team, and through it the story of a program and an era, you will find a wide and interesting variety of personal stories. Those players and coaches who became household names. Those who underachieved because they could not meet the demands of a highly demanding coach or because the glare of competition at that level and at that school was more than their maturity and talents could overcome. Those who overachieved, who pushed ability and athleticism and intelligence to the last level available and became a greater whole than their respective parts. And, then there are those who did all of the constructive parts properly and well, but through the vagaries of health in a high-contact, physical sport and the needs of a team to create depth and balance simply never got the opportunity to show the skills and hard-won athletic prowess that could very well have made their name known across a fandom and invited the glow of the national spotlight.

Just such a player was David Knapp, a schoolboy legend in his own right at Birmingham's Ramsay High School, a notable all-around athlete and a player who, as we will shortly learn, has a distinction quite rare if not unique in modern Alabama football lore. Even more, he is a warm and engaging man who I enjoyed getting to know during our interview and someone who was able to help me in my research for this book. He maintains a friendship with many of his teammates, was quick to shower praise and respect on them and their sacrifices and efforts, and was forthcoming not only with his stories and observations but also conversational and welcoming in casual acquaintance.

Our talk ranged across several areas, some of which are not necessarily applicable to this work, but one of the things that struck me most was his ability to look at his career at Alabama, involving not only positional changes but even moves from one side of the line of scrimmage to the other, alongside inopportune injuries that derailed his senior year and most likely denied him his chance to shine as a member of the 1972 team as an explosive and capable offensive weapon, with only a wry wistfulness and not a bitter cynicism. "What could have been" still lives in his memories, but is not a burden that prevents him from enjoying a successful life and retirement and the joys, which we both share, of watching our grandchildren grow and develop.

There are also the friendships and the relationships, some of which wander in and out of his memories like strands woven in a tapestry, from early days of YMCA football under the guidance of Coach Mutt Reynolds, whom he recalls as his favorite coach of all time, alongside future Alabama teammate Joe LaBue, to his time at Ramsay, on a team loaded with future SEC players which would come one point short of capturing a state championship in his senior season to a Sidney Lanier squad that used its significant advantage in numbers to stage a second-half rally, to his regular workouts today with three former teammates.

From his earliest high school days, Knapp was marked as an exceptional athlete. He was named a starter as a freshman at Ramsay even in the highly competitive Birmingham area and would go on to be named the Most Valuable Player in Jefferson County as a senior. He was tall for a running back of the day at six feet one, and with the advanced and efficient weight program at Ramsay, he combined strength and speed in a lethal package. The colleges in the South noticed him early on, and he began to be recruited by many of them during his sophomore year.

In answer to my query about what made him choose Alabama out of all his many suitors, Knapp replied. "It was my dream. Both of my parents went to Alabama, I grew up a big Alabama fan, and loved Pat Trammell. I used to sell programs at Legion Field to get into the games, or me and my buddies would climb on trucks and get in over the fence. Ken Stabler, Joe Namath, the chance to wear that Crimson jersey. It was what I wanted."

As an all-around performer at Ramsay, not only a running back but defensive back and punt returner, Knapp came to Alabama more ready to play than most freshmen, but the rules in place in those days prevented first-year players from participation in varsity sports. Knapp, who was not only still one of the faster players, but due to that excellent weight program stronger than most of his fellow classmates, even the linemen, led the freshman team in rushing and looked to be in line to join the offensive backfield in his next season.

However, due to the needs of the team and his tantalizing athleticism, he found himself at defensive back. The change was actually welcome to David, as it gave him a clearer path to playing time, which manifested itself in the opener in 1970 against an elite USC squad at Legion Field. The loaded Trojan roster spanked an outmanned Tide team that day, 42-21, and Knapp got a sobering welcome to the world of big-time college football. But, he persevered and progressed, seeing playing time throughout the season, and culminating with a starting assignment against Oklahoma in the Astro-Bluebonnet Bowl in Houston. He had some memories of that game, including one I found truly enlightening.

"We played in the Astrodome, at that time the largest enclosed stadium in the country. The Astros, the major league baseball team played there, and after we were there they were going to host an Evel Knevel show, so they just laid plywood down over the baseball field, then put this fake grass, like what you would buy at Wal-Mart, over that. It was hollow, like running between two-by-fours, and made the strangest sound. The 'grass' bunched up, it had rolls and places you had to step over. It was a strange game, and Oklahoma had some very good athletes, like Greg Pruit. They were like us, they would be very good the next year, but I had a really good game against them, and Jeff Rouzie, who would be a real leader on the defense the next year, was the defensive Most Outstanding Player. We had several sophomores who played well, and I thought that was good for us for the next year."

Not only did Knapp have a good performance in the bowl game, but he told me that he had a really good spring at defensive back, and was looking forward to being a contributor in the '71 season when fate and the decisions of Coach Bryant brought change to his life once again.

When Bryant called the team together for what many known as the "sink or swim" meeting to announce the switch to the wishbone, it was momentous for many of the players. Several of the men I interviewed for this book talked about the impact of that decision on their careers, from Terry Davis who found an offense that was highly suited to not only his talents but his temperament, to John Hannah, who was able to maximize his greatest assets.

But, for David Knapp, the move came attached to a switch back to the offensive side of the ball. The wishbone, with its three back, full house set, required numbers in the backfield, and once again the larger, agile Knapp was on the move, taking up the duties of a wishbone halfback alongside Musso, LaBue, Beck, and Jackson. This time, the move was not as welcome, as he had begun to feel at home on defense, and thought the schemes and techniques of Coach Bill Oliver were suited to him and his talents. But, as always a team player, he made the move. As he mentioned more than once during our conversation when discussing some of the moves and decisions of Coach Bryant, "What was I going to do, argue with him?"

And thus, David Knapp finds himself in a very select group, if not unique. In the modern era of college football, with free substitution and platoon football as the norm, he would become, in the opening game against the same USC Trojans, this time in Los Angeles, one of the few, if not only, players to start one game on defense and the next game on offense, because, as many now forget, when the Tide took the field at the Coliseum that evening and unveiled their new-look wishbone offense, it was Musso and Knapp at the starting halfback positions.

Knapp would continue to see action during the season, amassing 125 yards on 27 rushes and an important catch against Auburn. His best personal day was against Miami, replacing an injured Musso and gaining 81 yards on 12 carries.

"Of course, I wanted the ball more, but I did get to play a lot, and we were winning. I knocked a lot of guys down for Musso."

In watching the film from the Auburn game, you can see evidence for this assertion, with several crushing blocks which sprang the injured Musson for big gains. Knapp and his boyhood friend LaBue played a major role in Musso's notable senior campaign, and the expectation is that they would form a formidable tandem in the next season alongside the emerging Wilbur Jackson, but once again Life would intervene.

After a highly productive and promising spring and fall camp, Knapp seemed set for a senior year that would cap his experience in Tuscaloosa and finally let him show his paces, but one week before the opening game, a severe hamstring pull, an injury he had suffered before, derailed all of that. He would recover and play sparingly, but the dream of joining the ranks of the great Alabama running backs would never come to fruition.

As difficult as it was for him to make all the positional changes, it did provide me with the opportunity to get a unique and qualified opinion on the elements of the 1971 team. When I mentioned to Knapp my primary supposition, that this team, the changes in scheme and concept on both sides of the ball, the accumulation of talent, especially younger talent on defense that began to mature, and the return to a style of play better suited to Coach Bryant's mindset and philosophy, was instrumental in returning the Alabama football program to its place among the elites, his response was brief but emphatic. "I absolutely agree. It changed things a lot."

In discussing some of the particulars, he agreed with others that the hiring of Coach Oliver and his philosophy of zone-based coverages and technique over concept, combined with the blossoming of young talents on the defensive line, and in Knapp's words, especially the linebacker corps, helped the Tide to re-assert a dominance on that side of the ball which would shortly see them back among the most feared defenses in the nation.

"We just had so many good athletes. We had a lot of very good players sitting on the bench, or playing only a few snaps, guys who would have started elsewhere. The defensive line was really good, and the offensive line was the key, to me, in that first season. Sometimes you could go for three or four yards before you saw a defender, it was easy to run behind them, and Terry Davis was really quick, just built for that offense. We told him he was quick because he didn't want to get hit, but the offense really suited him. We had some guys who were better passers, who would have been more like Scott Hunter, especially Billy Sexton who transferred to Florida State, he could throw it as well as anyone I'd seen, but not everybody could run that wishbone. Terry could. The linebackers, Rouzie, Wayne Hall, Strickland, not much got past them. Rouzie was so tough, he would go back to the dorm after practice and do 200 pushups, everyone else could barely move. If you hadn't had that accident, hadn't crushed his foot, he would have been one of the great ones. And, we had good guys in the secondary, I tell you, Steve Higgenbotham would flat hit you. We just had so many guys."

What makes a man's career a success? I guess we all have to answer that in our own way. I spent an enjoyable February evening getting to know a man who got to achieve his boyhood dream of running onto the playing surface of Legion Field, wearing a Crimson jersey and playing for the legend that was Coach Bryant, who helped set the tone for the resurgence of the Crimson Tide football program, who made lifelong friends and memories, who played for all the stakes in college football, and went on to become a success in his life and career outside football, and whose pride and passion when discussing his University and his grandchildren were evident to anyone who cared to listen. Like most of us, there were the "wouldas" and "couldas", the injuries and position changes, maybe even a little bit of ill-timing, but the man I spoke with, who not only took time to offer me his opinions and stories, but more tangible help with research and contacts for teammates I had not been able to contact, who took time to compare "Pop" stories and encourage me on my path to finishing this book, and any others that may come in later times, was not a man obsessed or burdened by such things. No, I met a man who seemed to deeply appreciate the times that he had, the people that he shared them with, and the lessons that he carries with him even unto today. A man who "knocked a lot of folks down" for others, who made the moves when the team was in need, and who exemplifies all of those who contributed in ways that don't often make the headlines and the highlight packages and the memories of those in the stands. And, I am very glad I did.

Fourth Quarter

Fifteen minutes. An entire season of blood, sweat, effort, of triumphs and challenges, of national acclaim, and moments of anxiety, all came down to these final fifteen minutes of football. Two undefeated teams, two championship dreams, a Heisman Trophy winner and a player whose season was worthy of consideration, an overlooked but feisty quarterback who had found his opportunity, two veteran coaches with legacies on the line, and two fanbases who would live with the results of this game for 364 days, separated by seven points. Alabama had been the better team for the majority of the first three periods, but Auburn was still close enough to pull it out, and with Sullivan and Beasley, who had done just that time after time, that meant hope for those in blue-and-orange.

Alabama opened the quarter on the Auburn 27, and the weary Tiger defense, which would play over forty of the game's sixty minutes, girdled their pride and will for the stand of the game. And, immediately, they got the break they needed, as a simple FB dive resulted in a strange clipping call, which set the Tide offense back the full fifteen yards to the forty-two. Second and twenty-five, especially in a triple-option based offense, is not the best recipe for success, but Davis calmly returned to the counter option concept that had worked so well, and Musso, with a couple of physical blocks on the perimeter, exploded for a twelve-yard gain, finishing with his trademark authority.

The counter option again, this time to LaBue, looked promising early but gained only six yards, but this time Bill Davis was true from forty-one yards after Terry saved the attempt by snagging a high snap. Three points looked much bigger than normal at that stage of the game because now Auburn had to manufacture two scores, without much success to point to.

With 13:03 left, the Tigers and Sullivan had to be feeling some urgency. With their quick-strike capability, Auburn was still alive, but they had only the one big reception on the day, and the need to generate some movement was real.

What they got was a gut punch. After Gant crushed the kickoff through the endzone, the next drive started from the Tiger twenty, and Sullivan, facing once again pressure in his face, threw into the curl zone on his right, but linebacker Chuck Strickland diagnosed the play and stepped right into the pass. Following behind some good blocking, he rumbled down to the Auburn seven, giving Alabama a prime shot at putting the game away. A five-yard penalty moved Alabama back to the eleven, but once again, the counter option was executed to perfection, and three key blocks gave Davis time to pitch and Musso room to run, and the Italian Stallion stampeded into the promised land, going airborne for the last five yards. The PAT made it 24-7, and the celebration was on in the Crimson half of the stadium and in Tide households across the state.

Sullivan would face even more pressure for the last twelve minutes. The front four could mostly ignore the running game, and Sullivan was definitely in their sights. Sullivan escaped on first down and found Unger for three in the flats, but was unable to hook up with Robinette, and then missed Beasley by a surprising margin, almost throwing another interception because he could not set his feet to throw. Beverley launched another punt, and Alabama started from their thirty-eight.

The Alabama offensive line, which had controlled the line-of-scrimmage for most of the game, now began to exert themselves completely. Running plays, more directly aimed at the core of the defense, began to produce consistent gains, as the Auburn front showed the results of clock and field position control. Davis once again dropped the ball off to LaBue in the flats for a changeup, gaining twelve yards and almost more. Even an unfortunate Davis slip, which stopped a play with a chance for big results, couldn't stop the Tide, as he responded with a laser to Bailey for twelve yards. Davis converted and the clock continued to bleed away the Tiger's hopes, and the Tide seemed poised to apply the coup-de-grace. Another Davis to Bailey strike carried the ball to the three, Musso off right tackle inside the one, but then Johnny followed with his only misstep on this day, slamming into his lead blocker LaBue while gathering for the leap to glory and fumbling into the end zone, where it was recovered by the the shell-shocked Auburn defense. While the drive did not produce points, it did drain over seven minutes off the depleted clock, and now the regular season had less than five minutes left.

The reprieve was short lived. Sullivan found Henley for nine, and then Lowrey took advantage of a loosened defense to sprint for seven, putting the ball at the thirty-six. Sullivan, returning to the quick game which had once shown some promise, was rewarded with a tipped ball which was gathered in by a grateful Jeff Rouzie. The Alabama linebacker followed a convoy of teammates down the sideline and looked poised to finish with a touchdown, but Sullivan, a football warrior to the last, fought his way through the white jerseys and shouldered him out at the Auburn six.

His effort only delayed the inevitable. The counter dive found Musso galloping through a gaping hole for the finisher. One last successful PAT made the final 31-7, and the Crimson Tide, and their wildly successful head coach had answered their critics and re-established their position atop the SEC and Southern football in general. The gamble of committing to the wishbone, made even more dramatic by the decision to do so basically over fall camp, had paid off in a spectacular fashion, and, though no one present in Birmingham that day could possibly have known, would lay the foundation for a run of success and dominance that would eclipse even the accomplishments of the '60s.

An enduring image from the end of the game shows Sullivan, the epitome of class throughout his life, embracing Musso affectionately and congratulating his old rival on his personal and team success. Bowl games lay ahead for both teams, and Auburn would still be a factor in SEC football for the next two season, including the miracle finish of the 1972 Iron Bowl in the "Punt, Bama, Punt" game when a 16-3 Tide lead would disappear due to two almost identical Bill Newton punt blocks, both of which bounced directly into the arms of David Langer and resulted in a 17-16 Tiger win. But, on that fall day on the corner of Fairmont Drive, Bryant and his team pushed back the surge of Jordan and the Tigers, and it would not reach those heights for more than ten years when former Bryant assistant Pat Dye would revive the Tiger fortunes.

In the final analysis, Alabama emerged victorious from the 1971 Iron Bowl, that rarest of all Iron Bowls, because they were better on both lines of scrimmage, they were fundamentally more sound on defense, especially in terms of limiting Sullivan's scrambling and Beasley's runs after the catch, and because Davis was a magician in running the offense and throwing the ball. Additionally, as was discussed in the interviews with the defensive backs, a "tell" picked up by Coach Mal Moore the year before and added to the combination coverages and execution demanded by Coach Bill Oliver gave Alabama's defense the key to solving Sullivan and Beasley, as edge they would exploit beautifully. Add in the depth and quality of the Bama backfield, and the absolute heroic effort of Johnny Musso, who even hobbled with the bad toe, displayed all of his brilliance and humility on his final college turn at Legion Field. There are some who point to the distraction and euphoria of Sullivan's Heisman win, but the simple fact was that Alabama, with their ability to control the pace and tempo of the game and the resurgence of their defensive pedigree, was the better team, and it showed. The Tide was truly back, and even the defeat in Miami to an elite Nebraska squad would not dampen the season.

The Aftermath

Two major bowl games, two match-ups with dominant Big Eight teams, the same two teams who had played in the "Game of the Century" in Norman, Oklahoma, a thrilling game full of college superstars that ended with a dramatic 35-31 Cornhusker triumph. Auburn would face Oklahoma in New Orleans on New Year's Day, while Alabama and Nebraska would meet that night in what was effectively a national championship showdown in Miami.

Neither game would turn out to be particularly competitive.

Auburn, facing another wishbone offense, and one that was a bit more experienced and explosive with Greg Pruitt and quarterback Jack Mildren leading the way, opened the game with a long, methodical drive that lead to a touchdown, but only after a Mildren fumble at the goal line was recovered by the Sooners. A couple of Tiger turnovers later, the Sooners had exploded to a lead that would prove insurmountable. The Tigers, who were outclassed on both lines, played listlessly, and Sullivan would experience what was probably the least effective outing of his college career. The Sooners were the better team top to bottom, but the Tigers did little that day to make them earn it.

Similarly, in Miami, the Tide played uncharacteristically undisciplined football, with a multitude of errors on special teams and turnovers on offense, leaving an already challenged defense vulnerable to the efforts of Tagge, Rodgers, and Kinney. Several players would comment on the difference in preparation once the team arrived a full week early in Miami, from a difficult and dangerous practice field to the combined media and bowl obligations that seemed to constrict the on-the-field work to get ready for a truly talented Nebraska squad. Along with a dominating defense, especially up front, the Cornhuskers were the better team on that day, and Alabama made too many mistakes against such a powerful squad to keep the game competitive. An early 28-0 advantage became a 38-6 thumping that, while it decisively ended the championship dreams in Tuscaloosa, did not tarnish what was a highly successful and important season for both Coach Bryant and his program. Alabama was back in the national perspective and would remain so for the rest of the decade.

Auburn, as well, had much to celebrate. Coach Jordan had cemented his legendary status by proving that he could still helm a serious conference and national contender. The school enjoyed its first of now three Heisman trophy winners, and the Sullivan to Beasley combination made the Tigers a known commodity in the world of collegiate football once more. There was definitely some carry-over even with the graduation of the talented duo and many of their teammates, as the Tigers would surprise many in 1972 as the "Amazins" would finish with a 10-1 slate even without the dynamic duo, and after a chaotic 6-6 in 1973, would rebound one last time for their veteran coach with a 10-2 team in 1974, finishing with a tough loss to Alabama and a win over Texas in the Gator Bowl. The next year, 1975, would see a difficult 3-6-2 record and the retirement of Jordan, and the Tiger's program would struggle from that point on until the arrival of Pat Dye in 1981. However, the glory years of 1969-1971 still resound in the memories of those whose cry is, "War Eagle", and the evergreen images of Sullivan, Beasley, and their mates are primary elements of the Auburn football legacy.

Across the state in Tuscaloosa, it was the beginning of something very special. Alabama would lose a total of thirteen games between 1971 and 1980, with only four of those coming in the SEC. There would be three national titles, two other near misses, and eight conference championships. The wishbone would become synonymous with the Crimson Tide, and by the midpoint of the decade, the defense would again come to be annually considered as one of the best in the nation. Additionally, Bryant was able to return fully to his preferred mode of game control, and the success of his teams was a dominant factor in re-establishing the recruiting edge he had built in the 1960s. He had re-tooled and re-invented his program, and as his statement to McNair indicated, he could be proud of re-establishing the Crimson Tide as a pre-eminent national program.

That one game, on a cloudy day in Birmingham, was not the key to all of this, but it does serve as a symbolic point in which the Tigers reached mightily for the brass ring, and came up, as so many of their backs and receivers did that day, just a little short. Auburn entered the game with the name players, the pizzazz offense, and the building momentum of the new contender, but the Bryant formula of hard work, discipline, consistency, and selfless commitment to "team" turned them back in the game, and in the battle for control of not only the state but Southern football in general. In what is still, to this day, the rarest of Iron Bowls, with two undefeated teams, two Heisman-worthy players, supporting casts of talented and relentless players, and two coaches whose legacies would be shaped in this battle, the Alabama Crimson Tide showed the class, poise, grit, and determination their legendary leader demanded, and reclaimed their place in college football. One game can never truly encapsulate a season, just as one season can never truly tell the complete story of a program. But, in Birmingham, Alabama in the year of our Lord 1971, two teams competed for their pride, their ambitions, their legacies, and their direction, and the results of that day would reverberate throughout the decade, throughout the remainder of the century, and even today, some fifty years later, the echoes of that game can still be heard.

Author's note

Why does one write a book? There are several reasons, from financial dreams to a desire to share a viewpoint with the world to just the sheer joy of seeing your words in print. I began this particular journey due to the pleasure I had in seeing *Crimson Fraternity* in print, and the echo of the words of Richard Todd during our interview, when he mentioned that he flipped his commitment from Auburn to Alabama primarily on the strength of a conviction that even if he was not sure about running the wishbone, he was convinced that Coach Bryant was going to be a winner. Added to that was the quotes from Kirk McNair about his conversation with John Musso on the subject of Coach Bryant and the importance of the 1971 season, and his own conversation with Bryant in which the Coach called the resurgence of Alabama football in the 70s and 80s his biggest accomplishment. I have my own personal memories of that game, hazy I admit since I was very young, but strong nonetheless, and accented by the *Bama's Greatest Games* video series featuring the 1971 Alabama/Auburn matchup. Watching two very good teams, a collection of wonderful college players on both squads, and the collision of two of the legendary players in the history of both programs, along with two all-time coaches, makes this game, and that season, worth diving into.

But, as I began the process of research and interview for this book, I found something else. I found not only a pivotal season and game, not only a decade shaping conflict, but I found a group of men, the 1971 Alabama football team, who share a special and powerful bond that goes beyond my meager talents to describe. Teams create bonds, and it is not uncommon to find groups of players and coaches who share a connection long beyond the life of the particular season they experienced, but here I found something else, something more and grander. Some fifty years later, a group of men who endured a summer and fall camp that some who had the authority to do so reckoned unabashedly with the Junction days, who took the physical and philosophical leap with their living legend coach, ahead to the wishbone and back to the standards of toughness, physical conditioning, commitment and teamwork that had made his name a household one, and founded a legacy which would sustain the program throughout the remainder of his career and life, and still echoes in the successes of the Alabama Crimson Tide today. These are men, players, coaches, support staff, who not only occasionally meet to relive the old days, but who maintain a constant and continuous connection, who spoke with pride and clarity of that season and what it meant to them, the program, and their lives beyond Tuscaloosa. They are still intensely close, still engaged with each other and their legacy, and still striving to set and meet the standard they established in those long, dusty, challenging days in the Alabama summer heat.

And, I am forever indebted to them for allowing me to travel in that place for a bit. Each and every one of those men I had the privilege to speak to was gracious, forthcoming, and touched my life as they have so many other lives over the years. In writing my first book about the wishbone era quarterbacks at Alabama, I developed what I jokingly call a "coaches" interest in them, a protective nature that made me be very careful of their stories and their memories. In writing this book, the experience has been even deeper and more impactful. These men, their stories and their lives, have made an impression on me that will remain as long as I draw breath on this planet, and I am forever grateful for the opportunity.

I truly hope that many others read this work, not for any material return to its author, nor the satisfaction of reaching a larger audience with my words, but because I fervently believe that these stories need to be shared. I am, and always have been, a lover of stories, of the shared experience that comes from the artful relating of the thoughts, actions, and consequences of others. I ardently hope that in this book, I have faithfully and competently told the stories of these men and their season of resurgence.

For that team, for those men and others who could not or chose not to speak, their efforts and accomplishments should rightfully be remembered and respected. For those who would read, fans of football, the Crimson Tide, the era, or of the grace and power of the human spirit united in a team effort, these stories are a glimpse of what can be and should be, of how hard work, commitment, dedication, and self-less attitudes can create a monument of enduring beauty and inspiration. And, in these times, we certainly could all use such a vision.

Made in the USA
Monee, IL
14 July 2022

99718395R00108